Tasting Paradise

Restaurants & Recipes of the Hawaiian Islands

by Karen Bacon

COASTAL IMAGES

Tasting Paradise
Restaurants and Recipes of the Hawaiian Islands

Copyright © 1995 Karen Bacon
All rights reserved.

Cover art by Karen Bacon.
About the cover: All of the fruit pictured is grown in Hawaii.

Illustrated and designed by Karen Bacon.

Maps courtesy of Wizard Publications.

Published by:
Coastal Images
Post Office Box 1006
Kula, Maui, Hawaii 96790–1006
FAX (808) 878–3855

Please send any comments, questions, or suggestions to the above address.

Grateful acknowledgment made to Pali Jae Lee and Night Rainbow Publishing Co. for permission to reprint the excerpts on pages 11 and 12, from *Tales from the Night Rainbow*. Copyright 1988 by Pali Jae Lee and Koko Willis.

ISBN 0-9644327-0-6
Library of Congress Catalog Card Number 94-73936
Printed in Hong Kong

The author and publisher have made every effort to ensure that the information was accurate at press time; however we assume no responsibility for errors or inconsistencies. While the sources of the information contained in this book are believed to be reliable, changes in price, days open, menu items, etc. are inevitable and are therefore not guaranteed.

*This book is dedicated to
my daughter Cora for her
bright and loving spirit that
shines light on my life.*

Acknowledgments

Thank you to all of the chefs and restaurant owners for making this book possible by sharing your delicious recipes.

Great thanks to my friend Barbara Williams, author of *Cooking & Coasting*, for the concept and encouragement. You are an inspiration!

Many thanks to Andrew Doughty and Harriett Friedman for offering your valuable expertise, suggestions, and best of all, humor. I appreciate your generosity and helpfulness in many areas that were way beyond the call of duty.

My thanks to Martha Collins for your thoughtful input and for making the time in your busy schedule to proofread this book.

Much thanks and love to my family and friends who have offered their help, support, and interest, and have asked many times, "How's your book going?" You helped me keep the faith!

Special thanks to my brother Bob Bacon, my sister Carol Bacon Keith, and my brother in–law Rich Keith for generously giving your honest and valuable feedback. Thanks for being there for me! And thanks Bob, for going that extra mile when I needed you.

I would especially like to thank my daughter Cora who has watched with interest and patience, and has shared so much enthusiasm as this book was being created.

TABLE OF CONTENTS

TABLE OF CONTENTS

TABLE OF CONTENTS

Tasting Paradise

Warm sunny beaches, crystal clear blue water, the soothing sound of the waves crashing on the sand, spectacular views of lush green mountains, and a breeze blowing by softly scented with tropical flowers…Hawaii is known by many as paradise, a treat for all the senses. People from around the world are drawn to Hawaii's spectacular beauty and benevolent climate, adding to the rich and unique blend of the many different ethnic backgrounds already found in Hawaii.

In my travels around the Hawaiian Islands visiting the restaurants that are represented in this book, I enjoyed listening to the many beautiful accents I heard in my conversations with chefs and restaurant owners. The fabulous selection of enticing recipes and remarkable restaurants in this book are contributions from individuals representing many different cultures. It is truly rewarding to see them all come together in *Tasting Paradise* to offer you the opportunity to experience and share in this special and delicious cultural diversity while dining out in Hawaii, and while creating in your own kitchens at home. I invite you to share in the joy, warmth and fun that I experienced meeting these wonderful people and sampling so many delicious cuisines.

Selecting the Restaurants

A beautiful view, right on the beach, a unique and fun atmosphere, a lovely and elegant setting, a creative, innovative menu, great food…these are only some of the reasons that the restaurants in this book were selected. Most restaurants were recommended by word of mouth from people who live on the islands. I asked friends, friends of friends, restaurant owners, chefs and managers, and owners of Bed & Breakfasts where I stayed. It was valuable, and fun, to get recommendations from many different sources, and allows the book to feature a selection of restaurants that reflect a variety of tastes.

Although the information I've included in this book is from reliable sources, and will hopefully still hold true when you visit these establishments, in the restaurant business things can change from day to day and there are no guarantees. I recommend calling ahead before getting your heart set on something, just in case.

The Recipes

An extraordinary selection of mouthwatering recipes have been contributed. (Blackened Ahi with pineapple relish, Shrimp Won Tons with spicy sweet and sour sauce, Evil Jungle Pasta, Fajita Salad with avocado vinaigrette, Double Chocolate Bread Pudding with Kahlua creme anglaise…) Many chefs are sharing their most popular and delicious recipes, while others share specials that you will not find on their daily menu. You can enjoy creating and tasting, while choosing from a wealth of recipes representing Hawaii, Japan, Thailand, France, Italy, Mexico, and more.

New Cuisines

Each restaurant has selected the title for the type of cuisine they serve, which is shown at the top of the recipe page. Many of the cuisines will be familiar to you, and some will be new. Cooking is a creative and innovative endeavor, especially in Hawaii these days, where a culinary movement is creating the exceptional new cuisine of Hawaii that is being recognized around the world. By blending Asian and Western flavors and techniques, with the abundance of fresh ingredients available in Hawaii, chefs are creating exciting, innovative, and extraordinary culinary delights.

Many chefs are working with local farmers and fishermen to obtain exceptionally fresh, high quality ingredients. While developing direct relationships with farmers, chefs are requesting that special herbs and vegetables are grown for them, which have previously been unavailable in Hawaii. Chefs are also serving the traditional Hawaiian staples such as taro and sweet potatoes in new and creative ways, and are incorporating the wonderful selection of tropical fruits, such as papayas, pineapples, bananas, and mangoes, into incredible and enticing dishes. Superb entrées are being created using the amazing selection of unique and delicious fish that are available from the beautiful tropical waters that surround the islands. The popular and exquisite ahi is often eaten raw as sashimi for an appetizer (pupu), or seared and served with a mouthwatering sauce. Lobster, shrimp and salmon are also available fresh in Hawaii, thanks to the aquafarms that are gaining in popularity. The emphasis of this culinary movement is on fresh flavors and fresh locally available ingredients, making it health conscious as well.

As each chef creates his or her own unique approach to this new cuisine, many new names are being introduced to describe the cuisines. A few years ago twelve premier chefs created Hawaii Regional Cuisine, Inc. and are credited as being in the forefront of this movement. A few of the other cuisine names included here are Pacific Regional, Cross–Cultural, Euro–Island, and the more familiar Pacific Rim. The innovative culinary delights created by these chefs are truly a treat to experience.

How to Use This Book

This book will easily guide you to some of the best places to enjoy a meal out in Hawaii. It features a section for Kauai, Oahu, Maui, and Hawaii (also known as the Big Island). The map at the beginning of each section shows the general location of each restaurant followed by a page number. This will quickly guide you to the essential and interesting information about the restaurant including an illustration. A quick reference to cuisines is listed adjacent to the map so you can easily locate the type of food that sounds most appealing to you.

When you are not out exploring the best places to eat in Hawaii, *Tasting Paradise* becomes a guide for preparing delicious creations in your own kitchen using the incredible recipes that are featured in this book.

I hope you enjoy the delicious recipes, wonderful restaurants, and your own experience of *Tasting Paradise*.

Doing What You Love...

When I started on this project, which has turned into a journey, I knew it would be a wonderful combination of many of my skills and interests—art, writing, graphic design, travel, and of course, eating good food. There is something else that is very important to me that I did not realize would be a part of this project, but as I got farther down the path, I realized (to my joy) that it, too, was a part of this journey. It is a strong love, interest and fascination in the human process of individuals discovering their creative potential, and a way to make their living by doing what they love. In some of the interviews I did with chefs and restaurant owners, I was so pleased to see that many of them are "in their element", finding fulfillment and creative inspiration in their daily work.

I hope some of you will be inspired by the brief stories and messages that are shared in this book. Each individual expression of this process is so unique. This project is an expression of my own creative process and movement toward making a living by doing what I love. I was long ago inspired by Marsha Sinetar's great book *Do What You Love, The Money Will Follow*. It is less about money, and more about the human process of self actualization, and living a truly fulfilling and creative life.

This book, *Tasting Paradise*, is as much about people, as it is food. It's the people, the creative spirit, and the inspiration and feeling, that makes the food so flavorful and beautiful, and enables the dining experience to be so special. We must also all give our respectful thanks to the magical islands of Hawaii for providing us with all of this wonderful food and magnificent beauty, and to the spirit of *Aloha* that is shared by the people of Hawaii.

The Spirit of Aloha

Aloha means the spirit of love, and is commonly used as hello and goodbye. It also means compassion, kindness, and giving.

Aloha is being a part of all
and all being a part of me.
When there is pain—it is my pain.
When there is joy—it is mine also.
I respect all that is
as part of the Creator and part of me.
I will not willfully harm anyone or anything.
When food is needed I will take only my need
and explain why it is being taken.
The earth, the sky, the sea are mine
To care for, to cherish and to protect.
This is Hawaiian—This is *Aloha*! [1]

This beautiful message is shared in the book *Tales from the Night Rainbow*, by Pali Jae Lee and Koko Willis. The book was inspired by stories shared by their big grandma, Kaili'ohe Kame'ekua. As with all cultures, there are many different versions and interpretations of the history of the Hawaiian people. So much of what is commonly known is the history of the Tahitian people after they came to Hawaii (the *Alii*). But the true native Hawaiians that were here before the Tahitians came (pre *Alii*) have a very different history and philosophy of life. They taught through stories and parables (like the one above, and the one to follow, which were shared with children at a very early age). Another one of my favorite stories from *Tales from the Night Rainbow* is:

"Each child born has at birth, a Bowl of perfect Light. If he tends his Light it will grow in strength and he can do all things—swim with the shark, fly with the birds, know and understand all things. If, however, he

[1] *Pali Jae Lee and Koko Willis, Tales from the Night Rainbow (Honolulu, Hawaii: Night Rainbow Publishing Co., 1988), pp.18–19*

becomes envious or jealous he drops a stone into his Bowl of Light and some of the Light goes out. Light and the stone cannot hold the same space. If he continues to put stones in the Bowl of Light, the Light will go out and he will become a stone. A stone does not grow, nor does it move. If at any time he tires of being a stone, all he needs to do is turn the bowl upside down and the stones will fall away and the Light will grow once more." [1]

This is another beautiful and inspirational story. There is much we can learn from the Hawaiian perspective and by sharing the aloha spirit.

A Hawaiian Tradition

One of the Hawaiian traditions that is still practiced widely is the blessing ceremony. Most of us are familiar with the tradition or ritual of saying a blessing before we eat. The Hawaiian culture has a tradition of performing a blessing when something new is created, such as a boat or canoe, or a new home or business. It is similar to giving birth, and then blessing the newborn. I was intrigued and interested at how many of the restaurant owners, at some point in our conversation, mentioned the blessing ceremony that was performed for the opening of their restaurants. Impressed by how widely accepted and respected it is among the *haole* (white) people who now live in Hawaii, as well as those born and raised here, I began asking more questions about it. When I asked Chris Ayers, co–owner of Hanapepe Bookstore and Espresso Bar, why they did a blessing ceremony, she said, "Tradition, of course, and we wanted to make sure that everything was safe… After the doors are blessed, everyone who comes through the doors is blessed." She adds, "It's a nice way to say thank you to the powers that be."

Kelvin Ro, born on Oahu and owner of Kahala Moon, explained that a blessing helps "to ensure longevity, safety and prosperity, as well as community support…giving the best possible chance of success in a way that is allowing our spirituality to be a part of it—for peace of mind, and out of respect."

Part of the purpose of a blessing is cleansing, to clear the way of any conflict or bad experiences that may have occurred in the past, and then, to recognize what is new and bless it for the present and future, to bring goodness, safety, protection, and prosperity. The blessing ceremony is performed by a Priest or *Kahuna*. Each ceremony reflects the individual's own unique approach and style. Friends, family, and loved ones are invited and often a feast is offered by the host.

I spoke with Reverend Kealahou Alika who performed the blessing for Five Palms Beach Grill, I thank him for providing a written version of the blessing ceremony to share here as a way of adding insight and understanding for those of you who are interested in the blessing process:

Ho'ola'a Ho'okuakahi
A Blessing to Clear the Way

Five Palms Beach Grill
Sunday, June 24, 1994
Kihei, Maui, Hawai'i

Greeting—"E Ho Mai"

We look above
For wisdom to reveal to us the secrets of the words which are shared.
Come! Come! Come!
E ho mai ka ike mai luna mai e,
I na mea huna no'eau o na olelo e,
E ho mai! E ho mai! E ho mai! e.

INSIGHTS

Welina me kealoha ia oukou i keia 'auinala. We are here this evening to offer a blessing to *ho'okuakahi*, to clear the way.

Introduction

It was and is the belief of our Hawaiian *kupuna* that any new project or undertaking be preceded by prayer, often with ritual and feasting. In offering this blessing, we recall the act of the birth of a child. For the people of ancient Hawai'i the blessing was symbolized in the prayer known as "*ka oki 'ana o ka piko o ka hale*" or "the cutting of the navel string to the house."

The *piko* or umbilical cord was the symbolic name for the long thatching that was allowed to hang over the doorway, to be cut and trimmed when the *hale* or house was ready for occupancy. Because it was associated with the birth of a child, the ceremony was seen as celebrating the creation of a new structure.

Today, there is no thatch to be trimmed. Instead, we come to untie the *maile* [1] and in untying the *maile*, we symbolically celebrate the creation of something new.

Prosperity will come to this undertaking because of the quality and service you provide to all who come here. Prosperity will come to this undertaking because you are *pono* or just in your working relationships with one another.

Whatever your spiritual or religious traditions may be, each of you—by your presence—may offer a blessing for this occasion.
We come with the *lau ki* and the *pi kai*. The *lau ki* or ti leaf is to protect and keep safe. The *pi kai* [2] is to cleanse or purify.

The Blessing & Untying of the Maile

He pomaika'i nei au i keia o Five Palms Beach Grill *iloko ka inoa o ka Uhane o ke Akua.* We ask for a blessing for Five Palms Beach Grill in the name of the Spirit of God.

Aloha e! Aloha e! Aloha e!

Pau—End

We can greatly enrich our experience of the Hawaiian Islands if we share and learn about the culture, philosophy, and traditions. We can open our senses and hearts and quiet our minds to fully feel the beauty and spirit of the islands. We can share and appreciate the food and all of the individuals who have made it their livelihood, and sometimes passion, to grow, harvest, and prepare it for us.

What could be more blessed than food? Food, along with love, is our lifeblood. It brings people together and creates joy in our lives. Food is a creative expression, a way that we can share love and life with others!

---

[1] *Vines from the native Hawaiian shrub maile are strung together and used for this purpose.*

[2] *To sprinkle with seawater.*

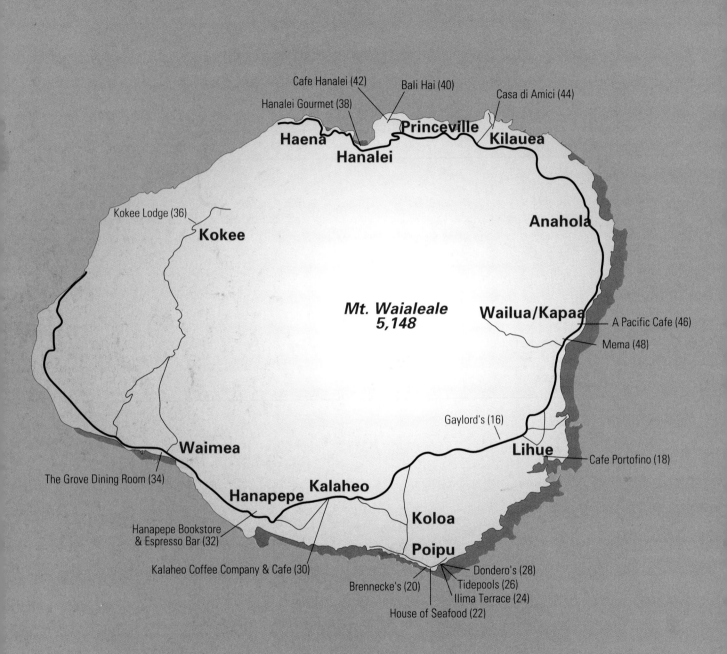

Cafe Hanalei (42)

Bali Hai (40)

Casa di Amici (44)

Hanalei Gourmet (38)

Haena

Princeville

Kilauea

Hanalei

Kokee Lodge (36)

Anahola

Kokee

Mt. Waialeale
5,148

Wailua/Kapaa

A Pacific Cafe (46)

Mema (48)

Gaylord's (16)

Lihue

Waimea

Cafe Portofino (18)

The Grove Dining Room (34)

Hanapepe

Kalaheo

Koloa

Hanapepe Bookstore
& Espresso Bar (32)

Poipu

Kalaheo Coffee Company & Cafe (30)

Dondero's (28)

Brennecke's (20)

Tidepools (26)

Ilima Terrace (24)

House of Seafood (22)

Kauai

The Garden Isle

Cuisines Featured

To be treated as a welcome guest in a beautiful plantation estate, go to Gaylord's Restaurant at Kilohana. The philosophy of owners Wally and Roberta Wallace is to treat everyone as they would treat guests in their own home. This creates a very gracious, warm and friendly atmosphere. The ambiance of Gaylord's is special and highly rated. Enjoy classical music while sitting in the lovely covered courtyard, surrounded by a beautiful garden, with a view of Kauai's lush green hills backed by Mt. Waialeale (the rainiest spot on earth). Occasionally a quaint horse drawn carriage will pass by, taking guests on tours of the 35 acre estate.

The 16,000 square foot historic plantation owner's home was built in 1935. You will find quality shops in the restored rooms and cottages.

Gaylord's welcomes families and is a wonderful place for special occasions including parties, weddings and receptions. It is very romantic in the evenings and they feature a very extensive wine list.

Their most popular dinner selection is Seafood Rhapsody—sautéed prawns, broiled lobster and fresh grilled fish. They feature homemade soups and salad dressings, and delicious desserts. Try the Lemon Almond Torte with Blueberry Coulis. It is fabulous!

Gaylord's is located just southwest of Lihue on the main highway. Lunch $7.00–$10.00. Dinner $14.00–$25.00 Weekend Brunch $8.00–$14.00. Reservations recommended. Open daily.

Baked Brie in Filo

1 Pound	Brie Round (Small)	2 Whole	Garlic Heads
8 Pieces	Filo	8 Tablespoons	Clarified Butter

Cut and trim brie so rind is removed. Let stand at room temperature for at least ½ hour to soften. Melt and clarify butter. Let cool. Chop off top of garlic. Roast at 350 degrees for ½ hour or until cloves can be squeezed out easily. Cut Filo so that it can be wrapped around entire brie one time. Lay one piece of Filo on flat surface, brush with 1 tablespoon butter. Lay another piece directly on top, brush with 1 tablespoon butter, and repeat until all 8 pieces are buttered and layered. Place roasted garlic which has been squeezed out of skin (at least 6 cloves) in the middle of Filo, and place brie directly on top. Wrap Filo around, folding so that Filo is tight against side of brie. Be sure the Filo overlaps on bottom so as to make a seal. Cut off any excess dough. Turn brie over so that the seam is on the bottom and garlic on top. Bake at 375 degrees for 25 minutes, or until golden brown. Serve with fresh sliced fruit and sliced french bread or crackers.

Chicken and Rosemary Fettucine

12	3 Ounce Skinless, Boneless Fresh Chicken breast pieces	¼ Ounce	Fresh Thai Basil (Purple) Leaves
2 Cups	Flour	8 Cups	Cream
24 Ounces	Artichoke Hearts (canned are fine)	2 Cups	Unsweetened Coconut Milk
24 Ounces	Fresh Mushrooms, sliced if necessary	Sprig	Lemon Grass
		½ Cup	Dry White Wine
1 Cup	Chicken Stock	3 Tablespoons	Clarified Butter
		48 Ounces	Rosemary Fettucine

Reduce the cream by bringing to a boil and boiling slowly for about 20 minutes to reduce to 6 Cups. Dredge chicken breasts in flour and sauté in clarified butter. Do not overcook. Remove from pan and set aside. In the same pan, add artichoke hearts, mushrooms and basil to hot pan, sauté until heated through. Splash with white wine to deglaze the pan. Immediately add reduced cream, coconut milk, sprig of lemon grass and chicken broth—simmer for 3 to 4 minutes—remove and discard lemon grass. Add pre–cooked rosemary fettucine and pre–cooked chicken breasts, toss to coat well and simmer about a minute to heat through. Arrange fettucine and 2 chicken breast pieces per plate, cover with sauce and garnish with purple basil or Italian parsley. Serves six.

CAFÉ PORTOFINO

(808) 245–2121 • 3501 Rice Street, Lihue, Kauai 96766

Chef Christian Riso, at Café Portofino, comes from four generations of Italian chefs. "Italian cuisine is very exciting, very romantic," he says. "I spend 12 hours a day in the kitchen and I love what I do. In Hawaiian it's Aloha, in Italian it's Amoré."

The owner, Giuseppe Avocadi, is from San Remo, Italy, and began working in restaurants at a very early age. What you experience in their restaurant is very authentic–from Giuseppe's accent as he greets you, and the fabulous fresh baked breads, freshly made pastas and specials, to the grand finale of authentic desserts (including fresh made Italian Gelato and Sorbets, and other tempting choices).

For dinner try the popular Scampi Con Fettuccine or Coniglio al Vino Bianco Olive Nere. On the lunch menu, sandwiches and a variety of salads are featured. Some vegetarian selections are offered on both menus, including a delicious vegetable lasagna made with fresh vegetables in season. Fresh fish specials are also offered daily.

The atmosphere is very pretty and comfortably elegant with linen table cloths and upholstered chairs. In the evening the candlelight creates a romantic ambiance, along with live jazz which is featured Thursday through Sunday evenings. Outdoor dining is available on the terrace, with a view of mountains and Kalapaki Bay.

Lunch Monday through Friday. Under $10.00. Dinner nightly. Entrees $9.50 –$19.00. Call for reservations.

Rabbit with Rosemary

2	2 Pound Rabbits, quartered		1 Cup	Olive Oil
1 Cup	Minced Garlic		2 Tablespoons	Flour
3 Sprigs	Fresh Rosemary		1 Cup	Chopped Onions
Pinch	Salt and Pepper		3 Cups	White Wine
1 Cup	Chopped Parsley		5 Cups	Vegetable Stock
			3 Tablespoons	Tomato Paste

Sauté the rabbit in a skillet with olive oil. Add chopped onions, garlic, parsley, and stir. After 4 minutes at a medium high temperature, add the flour. Stir well and add white wine with the rosemary. Let it reduce and add vegetable stock, salt, pepper, and tomato paste. Stir until it boils and finish cooking in the oven at 400 degrees for about 40 minutes. Serve with pasta cooked in the same sauce but add 1 tablespoon of butter. Serves six.

Mixed Grilled Fish

4	¾" Thick Slices Eggplant		4 Pieces	Red Snapper (6 ounces each)
4	¾" Thick Slices Yellow Squash		4	Scallops
4	¾" Thick Slices Zucchuni		4	Shrimp
4 Pieces	Sea Bass (6 ounces each)		8	Clams
4 Pieces	Salmon (6 ounces each)			

Sauce

3 Cups	Drained and Chopped Tomatoes		4	Chopped Garlic Cloves
4	Large Leaves Fresh Chopped Basil		1	Lemon (juice)
1	Red Bell Pepper, grilled and chopped		2 Tablespoons	Balsamic Vinegar
			Pinch	Salt and Pepper
			2 Cups	Olive Oil
			2 Tablespoons	Capers

Combine the above ingredients for sauce in a mixing bowl two hours before serving. Grill the vegetables and arrange them on a plate. Grill the fish and arrange over the vegetable slices. Each piece of fish is to be covered with the marinated tomato and pepper sauce. Serve at room temperature. Serves four.

Sitting up on the second story at Brennecke's, you are eye to eye with the tall palm trees and have a great view of people playing, surfing, and swimming at Poipu Beach Park. This is a fun, upbeat, and busy place.

Bob and Christine French opened Brennecke's in 1983. It was named after the world famous body surfing beach right next to Poipu Beach. They like to say, "Right on the Beach, right on the price."

Open air and casual, this is the place where you can come in right off the beach, still clad in a bathing suit and salt water. You can cool off with a refreshing tropical drink and get some great food.

They offer a nice salad bar all day. Delicious locally baked sourdough bread and fresh fish are also featured. On their Makai (Sea or Ocean) Specialties, Cioppino (Jumbo Shrimp, Fresh Fish, Crab and Clams in a spicy vegetable broth) is very popular and, they say, you'll never forget Brennecke's Signature Scampi. The Mauka (Inland or Mountain) selections include Prime Rib, Pork and Beef Ribs and New York Steak. They have a fun children's menu with lots of choices.

Lunch $6.50–$10.50. Dinner $6.50–27.00. Open daily.

Cioppino

⅓ Cup	Olive Oil
1 Cup	Finely Chopped Onion
1 Cup	Finely Diced Green Pepper
1 Cup	Finely Diced Golden Pepper
1 Cup	Finely Diced Red Pepper
1 Cup	Finely Diced Carrots
3 Cloves	Garlic, crushed
¼ Cup	Balsamic Vinegar
1½ Tablespoons	Fresh Parsley, chopped
1 Tablespoon	Fresh Oregano, chopped
1 Tablespoon	Fresh Basil, chopped
1 Tablespoon	Fresh Thyme, chopped
3 Pieces	Bay Leaves
¼ Cup	Red Wine
2 Cans (1 Lb. 12 Oz.)	Diced Tomato (or chopped whole tomatoes)
20 Pieces	Manila Clams–washed
1 Pound	King Crab, cut and trimmed/easy to open
1 Pound	Fresh Fish (Ahi, Ono, Mahi, etc.), cut into cubes
1 Pound (16–20)	Shrimp, shelled and cleaned
¼ Teaspoon	White Pepper
4 Cups	Stock
	Salt to Taste if preferred

Put all seafood with 1 teaspoon salt into 10 cups of boiling water. Cook for 1 to 2 minutes. Remove all seafood, set aside and refrigerate. Save stock and simmer for 10–15 minutes. Strain to have a clear stock. In a 10 quart stock pot (no aluminum please—use stainless steel, enamel, or glass) sauté in olive oil, onion, garlic, carrots, and red, green, and gold peppers. Add tomatoes with juice. Add wine, balsamic vinegar, parsley, oregano, basil, thyme, bay leaves and 4 cups of stock. Bring to boil. Reduce heat and simmer for 20 minutes. Add seafood to simmering vegetables and stock. Let simmer 10 minutes longer. Taste then add salt to your liking. Serve with hot crusty sour dough bread (good for soaking up soup). Serve in wide shallow soup bowls. Serves six to ten.

For Sauce for Clams, Scampi and Pasta from Brennecke's, see page 178.

THE HOUSE OF SEAFOOD

(808) 742–6433 • 1941 Poipu Road, Poipu, Kauai 96756

Fabulous seafood is what The House of Seafood is known for. The restaurant sits up on the second story amid the lush trees and greenery. There is a view out to the ocean and a birdseye view of the tennis courts below which offers great entertainment (sometimes humorous). The atmosphere is relaxed and fun, yet elegant.

The servers offer their own version of entertainment when they get to dramatically prepare the Ia Ula Ahi (flaming fish with garlic, shallots, white wine and enoki mushrooms) or the Flambé desserts. They like to have fun, are knowledgeable, and encourage guests to ask questions about the many creatively prepared (8–12 daily) fresh fish selections. The chef prepares each fish in a manner that best enhances its own natural flavor and texture, for example—baked in puff pastry, sautéed with a macadamia nut or orange cashew sauce, marinated or broiled, and many other delicious choices.

Dessert examples include Baked Alaska, Grand Marnier Soufflés, Crepes Suzette, Tortes, Mousse and more! You can place a special request for one of their incredible desserts, to be made especially for you, by calling one day ahead. Or you can choose from one of the 8 selections available each evening. They know how to please their customers! They feature an all American wine list with 80 selections. They offer a nice children's menu ($6.00–$13.00) which includes a variety of non–alcoholic tropical drinks. Dinner entrées $18.50–$38.00. Open nightly.

Ahi Luau

2 Pounds	Fresh Ahi (Tuna), cut into 8 portions		8 Ounces	Taro Leaves torn into 2" pieces (if unavailable, use fresh spinach)
¾ Cup	Flour			
1	Small Carrot, sliced julienne		4 Tablespoons	Coconut Milk
			2 Teaspoons	Whipping Cream
1 Stalk	Celery, sliced julienne		12 Ounces	Clam Juice
1 Teaspoon	Minced Garlic		4 Ounces	White Wine (Riesling)
1 Teaspoon	Ginger, fresh grated		Dash	White Pepper
5 Tablespoons	Butter		3	Green Onions (green part only, finely chopped)
¼ Teaspoon	Salt			

Bring clam juice to a boil, add taro leaves, cook for 5 minutes, and set aside. Sauté garlic, ginger, carrots, and celery in 2 tablespoons butter on high heat for 1 minute. Reduce heat to medium and add taro leaves with stock, coconut milk, cream, salt, and pepper, and cook for 3 minutes. Pour sauce into a serving dish and keep at serving temperature. Lightly flour the Ahi and sauté in 3 tablespoons butter for 1½ minutes, add the white wine, turn Ahi and sauté for 2 more minutes. Just before Ahi is finished, spoon the sauce onto individual plates. When the Ahi is finished, place two pieces on each plate, serving additional sauce on the side. Serves four.

Baked Papaya

2	Papayas		2 Tablespoons	Brown Sugar
1 Tablespoon	Cinnamon		1	Orange (juice)
1 Tablespoon	Sugar		½	Lemon (juice)
1 Tablespoon	Butter, melted		½ Ounce	Grand Marnier
2 Tablespoons	Butter			Vanilla Ice Cream

Preheat oven to 350 degrees. Cut the papayas in half lengthwise and seed. Sprinkle the sugar, brown sugar, and melted butter over the papaya halves. Place in oven proof dish and bake for 10–12 minutes in center of oven. While the papayas are baking, melt the butter in a sauce pan, then add the brown sugar, juice of one orange and half a lemon. Cook over low heat until you have a smooth consistency. Add the Grand Marnier and cool to room temperature. When papayas are done, let cool slightly. Place one scoop vanilla ice cream in each half and spoon over sauce. Serves four.

The Ilima Terrace has such a magnificent setting. You can sit outdoors right by a koi pond complete with two graceful Mute Swans. A waterfall rushes into the pond and lovely gardens surround it. Beyond all of this, you have a fabulous view of breaking waves and the gorgeous blue ocean at Shipwreck Beach. The interior architecture is grand with very tall ceilings, yet the open air atmosphere is pleasant and comfortable with Hawaiian music adding to the ambiance.

They offer a daily morning breakfast buffet for $16.50, and on Sunday, a brunch buffet ($19.75). Each evening they offer a theme buffet such as: Prime Rib (which includes roasted chicken and fresh island fish), Island night, Barbecue night, and Pacific Rim night. The dinner buffets are $23.95 and half price for children. Other menu items are featured as well. Popular items for lunch include their Lemon–Barbecued Chicken Salad with roasted shaved coconut, and their Mao Palai Noodles—stir fried chicken and Kauai made noodles with vegetables and Hon Dashi dipping broth. Dessert items include: Papaya cheesecake, Double Chocolate Strawberry Shortcake and more! Wine and tropical drinks are also offered. Breakfast under $10.00. Lunch $7.00–$14.00. Dinner entrées $7.00–$23.00. Open daily.

Chicken Papaya Salad

4 Ounces	Chicken (cooked)		¼	Papaya
2 Ounces	Bibb Lettuce		2 Ounces	Cantonese Vinaigrette
½ Ounce	Radicchio		1 Ounce	Shaved Coconut
1 Ounce	Leaf Lettuce			

Combine chicken, lettuces, and papaya. Add dressing and sprinkle shaved coconut over top.

Cantonese Vinaigrette

1 Teaspoon	Garlic, chopped		¼ Cup	Sesame Oil
1 Teaspoon	Ginger, chopped		1 Cup	Safflower Oil
½ Teaspoon	Dry Mustard		2½ Cups	Rice Wine Vinegar
1 Cup	Sugar		¼ Cup	Spring Onions, chopped
¾ Cup	Oyster Sauce			

In a mixing bowl, combine garlic, ginger, dry mustard and sugar. Mix oyster sauce into mixture until a smooth paste is formed. Slowly add oil. When dressing becomes thick, slowly add vinegar. Alternate oil and vinegar according to thickness until dressing is complete, then stir in spring onions.

Chicken Stir Fry

5 Ounces	Chicken (marinating is optional)		1 Ounce	Snow Peas
1 Ounce	Carrots, sliced		3 Ounces	Sauce (see recipe below)
1 Ounce	Celery		1	Scallion or green onion, diced, for garnish
2 Ounces	Won Bok		4 Ounces	Soba Noodles
2 Ounces	Bok Choy			Oil for frying
1 Ounce	Red Peppers			

Dice and marinate chicken. Slice all the vegetables and set aside. Then start preparing the sauce. Blanch and drain noodles. Heat the fry pan, make the noodles in round cakes and fry. Drain any excess oil. Heat wok and stir–fry chicken, drain, and remove from wok. Stir–fry the vegetables, then combine chicken, sauce, and cook. Place on noodles and garnish with diagonally cut green onion.

Sauce

¾ Teaspoon	Oyster Sauce		½ Ounce	Sake Wine
1 Teaspoon	Garlic		2 Ounces	Chicken Stock
1 Teaspoon	Ginger			Sugar to Taste
1 Ounce	Shoyu		1 Cup	Peanut Oil
½ Ounce	Rice Vinegar		¼ Cup	Corn Starch
1 Ounce	Mirin			

Combine the above ingredients and mix well. Then add 3 ounces to the chicken stir–fry.

Grass thatched huts sitting on a tranquil fresh water lagoon...the burning flame of the Tiki torch reflecting in the water while the sun sets—a tropical island ambiance is created at Tidepools. It has all the elements for a romantic tropical evening. ... can see Kanaka Ike Oke Kai (Knowledgeable Man of the Sea), a statue set in the picturesque tropical gardens. This was the only statue there that remained standing after Hurricane Iniki.

The food choices are great. Everything is fresh. The seafood and meat are hand filleted at Tidepools. They offer fabulous combination plates where you can choose selected main course items to combine, such as: Filet Mignon and Shrimp Scampi or Roasted Half Chicken and Half Lobster Tail. Their local style Poke is popular and made to order. Tidepools signature dish is Tidepools Mahi Mahi baked with braided bread wrapped around it on a slab of Kekaha Kiawe wood for great flavor! And don't miss the delicious desserts: Chocolate Macadamia Nut Pie, Apple Pie Tarts, Mud Pie...mmmmm.

Dinner nightly. Entrees $16.00–$36.00. Reservations recommended.

Coconut Beer Battered Chicken

½ Pound	Flour	Pinch	Salt
6 Ounces	Beer	Pinch	Sugar
6 Ounces	Water	2	Egg Whites
1½ Ounces	Oil		Shredded, Unsweetened
1	Egg Yolk		Coconut

Place flour in bowl, add beer, water, oil, yolk and seasoning. Blend. In separate bowl beat whites until stiff, but not dry and fold gently into flour mixture. Dip chicken strips in flour, shake off excess. Dip in batter, then into shredded unsweetened coconut, and fry in hot oil. Serve with Guava Sauce.

Guava Sauce

6 Ounces	Guava Jelly	1 Clove	Chopped Garlic
½ Teaspoon	Chopped Ginger	1	Cinnamon Stick
½ Cup	Water	2	Peppercorns
¼	Lemon, juice only	½	Lime, juice only

Combine all. Simmer ½ hour. Let sit 2 hours. Strain.

Charred Ahi with Papaya Relish

7 Ounces	Ahi, Cut into 2" X 2" X 6" blocks	1 Ounce	Blackened Seasoning
			Salt and Pepper to Taste
2 Ounces	Papaya Relish	Ounce	Soy Sauce
¼ Ounce	Sunflower Sprouts	2 Ounces	Soft Butter

Heat cast iron skillet or other heavy duty skillet on medium high heat for 5 minutes. Sprinkle blackened seasoning on Ahi. Place butter in skillet until melted. Place Ahi in skillet and cook on all four sides approximately 30 seconds each. Let cool. Slice into ¼" slices and arrange on a platter with sunflower sprouts and papaya relish. Serve with soy sauce.

Papaya Relish

1	Papaya, large dice	¼	Red Onion, medium dice
⅓	Pineapple, large dice	¼ Bunch	Cilantro, minced
½	Red Bell Pepper, medium dice	1	Lemon, juice only
		2	Limes, juice only

Mix all ingredients. Add salt and white pepper to taste.

Chef Gerardo Moceri of Dondero's discovered authentic recipes from the great old Italian chefs while working in a romantic 13th century castle in Italy. Authenticity is important to him and he has studied extensively. He has also cooked in Switzerland and France. In Italy, he was taken under the wing of, and apprenticed with Angelo Paracucchi—"One of the best and most creative chefs in Italy," says Chef Gerardo. He says that his own cuisine is "more health conscious than an Italian restaurant of yesteryear." He uses fresh Hawaiian ingredients, including lots of fresh herbs grown on Kauai for this creative regional Italian cuisine.

Dondero's offers a very elegant atmosphere in which to enjoy Chef Gerardo's culinary masterpieces. Beautiful Franciscan murals and 2500 hand painted seashells decorate the walls. A lovely piazza with beautiful gardens and the ocean nearby, is available for outdoor dining.

Specialties include: Involtini alla Saltimbocca—rolled veal with Prosciutto and Mozzarella, and Gamberoni Allo Champagne—sautéed Shrimp with Champagne Cream Sauce. Chef Gerardo recommends the Hazelnut Chocolate Crepe or the extravagant Tiramisu for dessert.

Call for reservations. Nice resort wear required (no thongs or tee shirts). Dinner nightly. Entrees $18.00–$27.00.

Rotolo di Papaya Con Ricotta

Pasta di Papaya

4 Cups	Unbleached Flour		Pinch	Salt
2	Eggs		2 Cups	Fresh Papaya Puree
4 Teaspoons	Olive Oil			

First, make a well with flour. Crack eggs into the well and put in fresh pureed papaya. Add salt and olive oil. Mix with a fork, working the pasta without breaking the walls of flour and slowly form a pasta ball.

Vanilla Sauce

1 Cup	White Wine		½ Cup	Butter
1	Vanilla Bean		1	Shallot
2 Cups	Heavy Cream			

Reduce white wine with shallot, add whole vanilla bean cut in half, and cream. Reduce until half, add butter slowly.

Vanilla Pine Nut Sauce

½ Cup	Roasted Pine Nuts		6 Ounces	Parmesan Cheese
¼ Cup	Walnuts		1½ Cups	Olive Oil
6 Cloves	Garlic			

In a blender, grind nuts, and slowly add garlic, cheese, and olive oil until a smooth paste forms. Add slowly into vanilla sauce and serve.

Ripieno for Rotolo

15 Ounces	Ricotta		1 Cup	Sundried Tomatoes, chopped
2	Eggs			
2	Egg Yolks			Salt and Pepper to Taste
½ Cup	Parmesan Cheese		1 Cup	Julienne Dry Papaya
3 Cups	Spinach, julienne			

Mix all ingredients together.

After making the pasta, roll it out on cheese cloth to a thickness of about 1/16" with a rolling pin. Spread evenly with ricotta mixture. Carefully roll up the pasta wrapping the cheese cloth around it. Wrap in aluminum foil and tie the ends tightly. Boil for 30–40 minutes. Remove, dip in cold water. Drain and let it rest for 10–15 minutes. Slowly unwrap, slice, cover with sauce and serve.

For Involtini d' Ono Alla Siciliana, Salsa di Pomodoro Arancia e Basilico and Ripieno Alla Siciliana (Sicilian Stuffing for Ono) from Dondero's, see page 179.

Kalaheo Coffee Co. & Cafe is the kind of place that every neighborhood loves and needs. This is exactly what John and Kristina Ferguson thought when they decided to create this great little place. They created the type of place that they like—great quality food at reasonable prices with a casual and friendly atmosphere.

My daughter, Cora

Well, a lot of people share their taste (including me!). Since the day they opened they have been busy serving happy customers who come back again and again.

John has been the executive chef at quality resorts. But what he really loves to do is start a restaurant from scratch, be involved in design, planning, construction, and then create fabulous food in the kitchen that he designed and helped build.

For breakfast their Wild and Wonderful Waffles are popular, and so is the Vegie Bagel Benny—grilled vegies topped with a poached egg and hollandaise sauce. Their lunch specialties are: Grilled Vegetable Sandwich marinated in fresh basil and set on their scrumptious fresh baked Focaccia bread. Also, Herb Chicken Breast, Pasta and Island Greens, or homemade soups and huge sandwiches on fresh baked bread round out the menu.

Their bakery items go well with their variety of espresso and cappuccino drinks (also available as thick ice cream shakes). Lunch and goodies served until 5:00 p.m. daily.

Breakfast $2.50–$5.00. Lunch $4.00–$7.00.

Scones

3–5 Tablespoons	Fresh Orange Juice	1 Tablespoon	Baking Powder
½	Orange, zest only	½ Teaspoon	Salt
½ Cup	Raisins/Currants	½ Cup	Unsalted Cold Butter, cut
3 Cups	Flour		into small pieces
⅓ Cup	Sugar	¾ Cup	Buttermilk

Egg Wash

1	Egg Yolk	1 Tablespoon	Milk

Sift flour, sugar, baking powder and salt into a bowl. Work butter into dry ingredients until nut size balls are formed. Make a well in the center, add wet ingredients and raisins. Work dough as in biscuits. Combine *without over working the dough.* Form into balls by pulling the dough and *don't over work.* (At this point, the dough can be frozen for future use.) Wash with egg wash before baking. Bake at 350 degrees for 20 minutes. Note: Other fruit may be used in place of raisins. Soak dry fruits in the orange juice or add fresh, frozen, or canned fruit in the same amount to the recipe in the same sequence. A slight adjustment of more flour may be needed if fruit is quite moist. Yields 10 medium size scones.

Kauai Carrot Cake

4	Eggs	¼ Teaspoon	Salt
1¼ Cups	Oil	2½ Teaspoons	Cinnamon
2 Cups	Sugar	2½ Cups	Carrots, grated
2 Teaspoons	Vanilla	8 Ounce Can	Pineapple, crushed, drained
2 Cups	Flour		
2 Teaspoons	Baking Powder	½ Cup	Coconut Flakes
1 Teaspoon	Baking Soda	1 Cup	Walnuts, chopped

Beat together first 4 ingredients until blended. Beat in the next 5 ingredients until blended. Stir in the remaining ingredients. Divide batter between 2 greased 9" tube pans and bake in a 350 degree oven for about 40 minutes, or until a cake tester, inserted in center, comes out clean. When cool, frost with Butter Cream Cheese Frosting. Each cake serves eight. Makes two cakes.

Butter Cream Cheese Frosting

½ Cup	Butter, softened	1 Teaspoon	Vanilla
8 Ounces	Cream Cheese	3 Cups	Sifted Powdered Sugar

Beat butter and cream cheese until blended. Beat in remaining ingredients until blended.

On the day of the solar eclipse in July 1991, Chris Ayers and Larry Reisor had the opening blessing for their fabulous Hanapepe Bookstore and Espresso Bar Cafe. It is located in the renovated old Igawa Drug Store. The soda fountain counter is now the focal point for their espresso bar. The atmosphere is fun, friendly, and comfortable. (The dress code there is: "No Ties".) They offer many delicious examples of how vegetarian food can be flavorful, exciting, and exotic. Guests tell them that they have never tasted so many different flavors in their food. And, as Chris likes to say, "The nicest thing about our restaurant is that nothing has to die for you to eat here."

The ingredients are fresh, including organic produce from local farmers. Their dinner menu is new each week based on what types of fresh ingredients are available. An example: Portabella Mushrooms Wrapped in Phyllo, served with a Raspberry Cabernet Sauce, with a beautifully exquisite presentation. For dessert, try their delicious Tira Misu. Lunch offers a variety of exotic garden burgers, homemade soups and salads, and a daily pasta special. For breakfast—pancakes, waffles, and more. Breakfast and lunch $3.00–$7.75, served Wednesday through Saturday. Sunday brunch. Dinner entrées $13.00–$16.00, served Thursday through Saturday, call for reservations

The bookstore area features Hawaiiana and locally made artistic products.

Gorgonzola & Sweet Potato Ravioli with a Lemon Basil Butter Sauce
—Chef Greg Forker

2 Pounds	Sweet Potatoes		4	8½" X 11" Pasta Sheets or
6 Ounces	Gorgonzola Cheese (or			2 Packages of Wonton Pi
	Blue Cheese), crumbled		2	Egg Whites
½ Teaspoon	White Pepper		2 Tablespoons	Water

Place sweet potatoes on baking sheet in a 375 degree preheated oven for 1 hour or until soft to touch. When cooled, remove skin and coarsely mash, then add cheese and white pepper. Place pasta or wonton pi wraps on a flat surface. Allow 2½" X 2½" per ravioli. Brush pasta with egg wash mixture on all edges. Place 1 heaping teaspoon of potato/cheese mixture per ravioli. Fold pasta squares in a triangle shape, or cover each one with another square and cut with a round pasta cutter. Be sure to press all edges together firmly. Set ravioli to the side until ready to cook. Bring 8 quarts of water to a simmer.

Lemon Basil Butter Sauce

1 Teaspoon	Minced Shallots		¼ Cup	Fresh Lemon Juice
2 Ounces	Lemon Basil or Regular		2 Tablespoons	"100% Real" Maple Syrup
	Basil if Lemon Basil is not		8 Ounces	Unsalted Butter
	available		½ Teaspoon	White Pepper
6 Ounces	White Wine			

In a medium size sauce pan over medium low heat, add first 5 ingredients. Reduce to ½ volume. Have butter cut into small chunks at room temperature. Add butter a little at a time, using a whip until all is incorporated. Add white pepper to taste.

To cook ravioli, place ½ of them in simmering water and cook for 4 minutes. After they have floated to the surface, remove with a slotted spoon and drain. Repeat method for remaining half. Top with sauce and enjoy. The sweet/tart taste of the lemon basil sauce complements the flavors of the sweet potatoes and gorgonzola cheese. Yield: 4–6 ravioli per person.

For Poached Pears on Puff Pastry with Cinnamon Cream Anglaise and Warm Port Sauce from Hanapepe Bookstore & Espresso Bar Cafe, see page 180.

The first time I ate at The Grove, I sat with my Dad and Aunt on the lanai and felt the warm breeze blowing by. It was my Dad's first trip to Hawaii. As we looked out into the grove of tall palm trees, past the historic plantation cottages and out to the ocean, my Dad said, "This is exactly how I'd always imagined Hawaii to be". They have captured a timeless feeling or essence of Hawaii, and have combined it with a fresh, innovative approach to local cuisine.

Aloha is felt there, and you never know when there might be an impromptu hula by one of the staff or guests. Live music is featured on the weekends. On most Friday and Saturday evenings you can enjoy the outstanding authentic Hawaiian music of The Kahelelani Serenaders from Niihau.

The Grove has a very pleasant cafe area where lunch and drinks are served. It's a great place to stop and enjoy a sandwich, salad, or local style plate lunch on the way to or from Waimea Canyon. If you're coming by on Sunday, stop in for their Sunday Champagne Brunch. Brunch and dinner are served in the nice, airy dining room or out on the lanai.

The menu provides a variety of fresh fish, salads, and local favorites, such as Waimea Chicken Tempura with Spicy Sweet-n-Sour Lilikoi Sauce (recipe at right) and Hawaiian Seafood Stirfry. To top off your delicious meal, try their "famous" Kikiaola Sand Pie, created by Executive Chef Bernal Fernandez.

Lunch, Tuesday to Friday, $6.00–$10.00. Sunday brunch.
Dinner, Tuesday to Saturday. Most full dinners are
$13.00–$20.00. Reservations recommended.

Waimea Chicken Tempura with Spicy, Sweet–n–Sour Lilikoi Sauce

3 Pounds	Boneless, Skinless Chicken Breast (cut each piece into 4–5 strips)	8 Slices	Pineapple

Tempura Batter

1 Cup	Flour	¼ Cup	Ice Water (more if needed)
1	Egg	1–2 Drops	Yellow Food Coloring
Pinch	Salt		

Mix all together in stainless steel bowl, then set aside.

Spicy Sweet–n–Sour Lilikoi Sauce

1 Cup	Water	1 Cup	Sugar
1 Teaspoon	Chili Paste, or any type of Hot Peppers (Optional Tabasco Sauce)	¼ Cup	White Vinegar
		Pinch	Salt
1 Cup	Lilikoi Concentrated Juice		Cornstarch and Water Solution

Bring all ingredients to a boil, except for cornstarch solution. Thicken slightly with cornstarch solution.

For preparation, heat oil at 350 degrees. Dip chicken strips in batter, one by one, and deep fry in oil until golden brown, making sure chicken is cooked on the inside. Place chicken on paper towel to remove excess oil. Grill pineapple slices, place on a plate. Arrange chicken strips on the pineapple and ladle sauce over chicken. Garnish with black sesame seeds. Serves seven to eight.

Kikiaola Sand Pie

Crust

2 Cups	Macadamia Nuts, chopped	2 Tablespoons	Brown Sugar
⅓ Cup	Flour	¼ Cup	Butter, melted

Mix ingredients together well and press firmly into a 9–10" cheesecake spring pan. Bake at 275 degrees for 7–9 minutes and chill for 10 minutes.

First Layer

Vanilla Ice Cream, about 1" thick

Second Layer

Kona Coffee Ice Cream, about 1" thick		½ Cup	Kahlua Liqueur

Mix the vanilla ice cream until soft. Pour in pan and freeze for about an hour. Mix Kona coffee ice cream and Kahlua until soft. Pour on top of the frozen vanilla ice cream. Freeze for another hour or overnight. When the ice cream is hard, release the spring pan, and take out the frozen pie. Cut into 16 pieces, and top with whipped cream before serving.

KOKEE LODGE

(808) 335–6061 • Kokee State Park, Kauai 96796

Just past the spectacular Waimea Canyon, which is also known as the Grand Canyon of the Pacific, you will find beautiful Kokee State Park. At about 3,600 feet elevation, the air is usually much cooler than the rest of the island. There are forests and lots of great hiking trails. Past the Lodge, at the very end of the road, a breathtaking view of Kalalau Valley and the Pacific Ocean awaits you. The view is often covered with clouds. It can take patience to wait for a clearing, but the reward is worthwhile.

Colorful roosters will greet you as you walk up to Kokee Lodge for a casual, light breakfast or lunch. They offer sandwiches, Portuguese Bean Soup ("local soul food"), and chili. They have great mud pie for dessert, which they call Alakai Swamp Pie (Kona Coffee ice cream, chocolate cookie crust, with macadamia nuts, fudge and whipped cream–so good!), a nice treat after hiking the Alakai Swamp trail. Mai Tais, other cocktails, beer and wine are also served.

Their gift shop features many Hawaiian made products, including soap made by a friend of mine on Kauai. The Kokee Natural History Museum is also interesting to check out. You can even rent a cabin to stay in overnight. (Call ahead for reservations.) Residents of Kauai will often rent a cabin at Kokee for a weekend get away and a nice change of pace.

Light breakfast and lunch daily. Under $6.00.

Lilikoi (Passion Fruit) Chiffon Pie

1	Baked, Nine–Inch Pie Shell	⅔ Cup	Sugar
4	Eggs, separated	2 Teaspoons	Knox Gelatin
⅔ Cup	Lilikoi Concentrate (do not dilute)	2 Tablespoons + 2 Teaspoons	Water

In a heavy sauce pan whisk together the egg yolks, lilikoi concentrate, ⅓ cup sugar, water and gelatin. Cook over medium heat, stirring constantly, until gelatin and sugar dissolve. Cool. Beat egg whites until fluffy. Fold in remaining ⅓ cup sugar. Fold lilikoi mixture into egg whites until blended. Pour into baked pie shell and chill until firm. Top with whipped cream.

Portuguese Bean Soup

8 Ounces	Dry Kidney Beans	12 Ounces	Hot Portuguese Sausage, sliced
1 Pound	Ham Hock	1 Small	Cabbage, chopped
1 Pound	Soup Bone	1 Clove	Garlic, minced
1	Onion, chopped	1 Bunch	Parsley, minced
2 Whole	Cloves	3	Peppercorns
½ Pound	Celery, sliced	1	Bay Leaf
2–3	Carrots, sliced	8 Ounces	Tomato Sauce
1	Salad Potato, cubed		
½	Green Pepper, minced		

Soak beans overnight in 1 quart water and 1 teaspoon salt. Drain. Add remaining ingredients—except sausage and cabbage—with 8 cups water. Simmer, partially covered, four to five hours, adding water as necessary. Add sausage and simmer 30 minutes. Remove ham hock and soup bone. Pick off meat and return to stock pot. Refrigerate to degrease, if possible. Reheat, add cabbage and more water, if necessary, and simmer 30 minutes.

There is "life after dark in Hanalei!" The Hanalei Gourmet is a busy hangout for residents and visitors alike. They feature live music six to seven nights a week, including jazz, rock and roll, rhythm and blues, and a Hawaiian jam on Sundays. In the afternoons they have a sports bar atmosphere.

They are open for breakfast offering homemade muffins and danish, and a few heartier breakfast items. Tim Kerlin, the owner, (known as Big Tim) is proud of the creative and talented chefs there who create daily specials including Thai, Gourmet Mexican, Fresh Fish dishes and more! On their menu, the Roasted Eggplant Sandwich is very popular with a delicious and unique combination of flavors. Great appetizers include the "Old Bay " Shrimp Boil and the Artichoke Dip. You can stock up on sandwiches and goodies for a beach picnic at the deli area and don't forget the yummy carrot cake and other scrumptious desserts, made by Suzi of Suzi's Date Bar.

The old school house, where the Hanalei Gourmet is located, was almost destroyed by a bulldozer when Gaylord Wilcox stepped in to save it. He bought it for $1.00, signed an agreement that he would have it restored to its original form, and moved it (in 7 pieces) to its present location.

Open daily for breakfast, lunch and dinner. Usually well under $10.00 (specials are sometimes more).

Island Style Shrimp and Sweet Potato Fritters with a Spicy Macadamia Nut Dipping Sauce
—Chef Gregory Jon Foster

Sauce

2 Cloves	Garlic, crushed	¼ Cup	Nuoc Mam (Vietnamese Fish Sauce)
1	Fresh Red Chili Pepper, finely minced	3 Tablespoons	Toasted Macadamia Nuts, ground
2 Tablespoons	Sugar		
2 Tablespoons	Lime Juice	2 Tablespoons	Chopped Fresh Cilantro
¼ Cup	Rice Vinegar		

Combine sugar and garlic in a mortar and pestle, grind to a paste. Mix in lime juice and vinegar. Stir to dissolve sugar. Combine remaining ingredients. Stir well. Let stand at room temperature for 1 hour to combine flavors. Note: This sauce is somewhat pungent. A few tablespoons of water may be added to achieve desired taste.

Fritters

24	Shrimp, head on preferred	1 Tablespoon	Madras Curry Powder
1 Tablespoon	Fish Sauce (Nuoc Mam)	1	Large Sweet Potato
4	Cloves Garlic, minced	¼	Red Onion, julienned paper thin
2 Cups	Flour		
2 Tablespoons	Dark Brown Sugar	2	Scallions, finely sliced
1 Tablespoon	Salt	3 Tablespoons	Fresh Cilantro, coarsely chopped
2 Teaspoons	Baking Powder		

Peel the shrimp, leaving the heads and tails on 16 for a garnish. Cut the remaining shrimp into pieces. Marinate the shrimp in the fish sauce and garlic.

Combine the flour, brown sugar, salt, baking powder and curry powder in a bowl. Make a well in the center and whisk in 1–1¼ cups cold water to form a light batter.

In a larger bowl, combine the red onion, scallions and cilantro. Peel the sweet potato, slice into paper thin rounds, then cut the rounds into a fine julienne. Combine with the onion and scallion mixture. Add the chopped shrimp and about ¾ of the batter. Mix well. Heat 2–3 inches of peanut oil in a wok to 370 degrees. Form the fritter mixture on a wide spatula, about 2 tablespoons batter per fritter. Place a whole shrimp in the center and press firmly to secure. Take a long thin knife and gently slide the fritters into the oil and fry, turning once, until golden brown. Transfer to a platter lined with paper towels and keep warm in a 375 degree oven until ready to serve. Serve the fritters on bibb lettuce with the dipping sauce. Yield: 16 cakes (approximately).

For Smoked Salmon and Potato Cakes with Dill Cream from Hanalei Gourmet, see page 181.

Ho'o Kipa is part of the philosophy at Bali Hai Restaurant. It means hospitality, smiles, and aloha that comes from the heart. The staff is taught history and stories of the Hawaiian culture to share the specialness and deeper meaning of Hawaii with guests. That specialness is part of what you feel sitting in the open air atmosphere, looking out over beautiful Hanalei Bay, surrounded by majestic mountains.

Executive Chef, Geoff Anderson, planted an organic herb garden on the premises of Hanalei Bay Resort, where the restaurant is located. Guests are welcome to tour and taste in the garden, which includes 43 herbs and 23 chili peppers. Papayas, bananas, guavas, and bread fruit are also grown on the premises. All of these very fresh ingredients are used to prepare superb dishes. Everything is made from scratch, including their own granola, muffins, and delicious rolls served with dinner. Taro hash browns and Poi pancakes are fun to try for breakfast, among many other delicious choices. Lunch offers unique salads (Spicy Beef Salad, Smoked Tofu Salad), sandwiches, and entrées. For dinner, their signature item is Salmon Bali Hai—so delicious it melts in your mouth! Fresh fish of the day includes your choice of sauce—Thai Sesame, Papaya Salsa, Banana Curry, or Drambuie Herb Butter.

Open daily. Breakfast $4.00–$12.50. Lunch $8.00–$13.50. Dinner $17.00–$26.00. Reservations recommended. Ask for directions from the Princeville entrance information booth.

Bali Hai Salmon

Duxelle

12 Ounces	Chopped Cooked, Frozen Spinach, thawed, drained	1 Ounce	Pernod (Anise Liqueur)
8 Ounces	Cream Cheese (room temperature)	½ Teaspoon	Salt
		¼ Teaspoon	White Pepper
1	Onion, minced	1 Tablespoon	Olive Oil
1 Tablespoon	Capers, minced	1 Teaspoon	Worcestershire Sauce

Heat oil in a sauté pan over medium high heat. When hot, add onion. Sauté until translucent. Add capers and toss several times. Deglaze with the Pernod. Add spinach and warm. Do not overcook. Add cream cheese, Worcestershire, seasonings, and mix. Keep warm.

Beurre Blanc

1	Small Shallot, minced	½	Lemon
1 Cup	Medium Body White Wine	¼ Pound	Butter (cut in cubes)
¼ Cup	Heavy Cream		

In a saucepan, reduce shallot and wine. Add cream and simmer to a large bubble consistency. Add squeeze of lemon and return to large bubble consistency. Stir cubed butter in by thirds. Remove from heat. Hold in double boiler over low heat.

Puff Pastry

8	5" X 5" Puff Pastry Sheets	2 Tablespoons	Water
1	Egg		

Mix egg and water until smooth. Cut pastry to shapes making tops to match with slightly larger bottoms. Lightly brush tops of pastry sheets with egg mixture. Place on sheet pan and bake at 350 degrees until golden brown, approximately 10 minutes depending on product.

4	6 Ounce Salmon Fillets (best if approximately the same size for equal cooking times)

Dust with seasoned flour (salt and white pepper). Place into a sauté pan preheated with clarified butter or olive oil. Brown lightly (tops first). Turn. Top each fillet with an equal portion of Duxelle and place pan into a 350 degree oven. Cook until firm but still moist. Place salmon fillet and Duxelle between (cooked) pastry sheets. Place most of sauce underneath each serving and a small amount over the top. Garnish with fresh herbs and lemon. Serves four.

For Peanut Chicken Breast with Curry Sauce from Bali Hai, see page 182.

Cafe Hanalei offers an unforgettable experience and a treat for all the senses. The interior architecture and atmosphere are beautiful and very elegant yet still comfortable and friendly. When you are sitting on the lanai, with breathtaking views of Hanalei Bay and spectacular mountains, enjoying fabulous food and great service…who could ask for more? That's how it feels.

The Executive Chef, Daniel Delbrel, uses many locally grown products to create a local flavor, a "taste of Hawaii". And, he shares, "You have to cook with your heart and feeling, you must put passion in your food." Examples include: Hawaiian Swordfish with sautéed spinach and a lemon thyme sauce, Grilled Sake Marinated Shrimp and Sea Scallops with chunky avocado tomato salsa, Roasted Rack of Lamb served with a papaya and star fruit mint salsa, and many other dishes with Thai and Japanese influences (including the Thai Style Chicken and Beef Satay).

Cafe Hanalei features outstanding buffets. Friday features Seafood. My favorite is the Sunday brunch buffet where an incredible selection of delicious food is presented. Items including fresh fish, omelets, crepes, and waffles are prepared fresh to your liking, and there are many exquisite desserts. Indulge!

It's a great place to feel special and enjoy yourself any time of day. The mornings are beautiful, the sunsets are magnificent. Open daily. Breakfast $5.00–$23.00. Lunch $8.00–$18.00. Dinner entrées $15.00–$33.00. Reservations recommended.

Smoked Opah (Moonfish) Mousse with Sweet Hawaiian Corn Relish

8 Ounces	Smoked Opah (Moonfish) or any smoked white fish		2 Ounces	Sour Cream
3 Ounces	Cream Cheese		1	Lemon, juice only
				Salt and Pepper to Taste

Puree the fish in a food processor. Add sour cream, cream cheese, and lemon juice. Season with salt and pepper, and chill.

Sweet Corn Relish

6 Ounces	Fresh Sweet Corn Kernels		1 Ounce	Maui Onion
1 Ounce	Each Red and Green Bell Pepper, finely diced		1 Ounce	Tomato, diced, no seeds
			1 Teaspoon	Chives, finely cut

Mix all ingredients together.

Dressing

1 Ounce	Rice Vinegar		1 Teaspoon	Red Curry Paste
1 Teaspoon	Minced Garlic		2 Ounces	Peanut Oil
1 Teaspoon	Dijon Mustard			

Mix ingredients then add corn relish. Spoon corn relish and mousse on plate. Serve with toasted French bread. Serves eight.

Steamed Hawaiian Snapper with Ginger, Cilantro and Shiitake Mushrooms

7 Ounces	Snapper		1 Tablespoon	Cilantro Leaves
1 Teaspoon	Ginger, fine julienne		1 Tablespoon	Hot Peanut Oil
1 Teaspoon	Green Onion, fine julienne		1 Tablespoon	Light Shoyu Sauce
1 Tablespoon	Shiitake Mushroom, sliced			

Place fish in a steamer and cook for about 8–10 minutes depending on the thickness of fish. Place steamed fish on plate. Place green onion, shiitake, ginger, and cilantro on top. Pour hot peanut oil and drizzle shoyu sauce over dish. Serve with steamed potato.

There is a "House of Friends" in the little town of Kilauea that is a pleasant surprise to many. Casa di Amici (House of Friends, of course) brings visitors and residents back many times to enjoy the romantic ambiance and fine Italian cuisine. You can listen to live solo piano seven nights a week in the friendly, open air atmosphere. Owner, Patrick Tuohy teams up with Chef Randall Yates to create a memorable dining experience and "to give everyone something they want to come back to." Casa di Amici has been written about in Bon Appétit, Gourmet Magazine and Travel and Leisure.

Chef Randall Yates comes from a varied background but has found his love in being a chef. An honors graduate from the California Culinary Academy, he places a great emphasis on using only the finest ingredients, with quality as his highest priority.

Their signature appetizer is Bacio Di Amicizia (The Kiss of Friendship)—Boursin cheese wrapped in a phyllo crust and served with house sauce. On their menu they feature many different pastas which you can combine with the sauce of your choice. An example of one of their nightly specials is Salmon and Prawns in a cognac sauce on fettucine. They offer many decadent desserts and a wide selection of Italian and domestic wines.

Dinner nightly. Entrees $12.00–$24.00. Reservations please.

Chicken Gorgonzola

5 Ounces	Chicken Breast, skinless/boneless		¼ Cup	Chopped Fresh Tomato
2 Tablespoons	Olive Oil		1 Teaspoon	Chopped Fresh Sage
	Flour for Dredging		⅓ Cup	Heavy Cream
4 Ounces	Chicken Stock			Salt and Pepper to Taste
5 Tablespoons	Gorgonzola Cheese		5 Ounces	Warm, al Dente Farfalle Pasta

Flour chicken. Sauté chicken in hot olive oil just to color lightly. Remove from pan, cut into strips. Pour off olive oil. Add chicken stock, gorgonzola, tomatoes, sage and heavy cream. Return chicken to pan and reduce over high heat until you reach sauce consistency. Add warm pasta. Serve immediately. Serves one.

Shrimp in Sun–Dried Tomato Pesto

6	Large Shrimp		¼ Cup	Cream
3 Tablespoons	Sun–Dried Tomato Pesto (recipe below)		½ Cup	Mixed Red, Gold, & Green Bell Peppers, cut julienne
1 Tablespoon	Hazelnut Oil		5 Ounces	Al Dente Pasta
4 Ounces	Fish Stock or Clam Juice			

Add all ingredients except shrimp and pasta to sauté pan. Mix over high heat until bubbling. Add shrimp. Cook 45 seconds on each side. Toss with warm pasta. Serves one.

Sun–Dried Tomato Pesto

3 Ounces	Sun–Dried Tomato		2 Teaspoons	Garlic Puree
2 Ounces	Salami, chopped		½	Lemon, juice only
2 Tablespoons	Dijon Mustard		½ Cup	Olive Oil
2 Tablespoons	Fennel Seed		¼ Cup	Pernod

Add all ingredients to a food processor except olive oil and Pernod. Turn on machine, slowly add Pernod, then olive oil in a thin stream. Process until smooth. Toss with warm pasta. Serves one.

A Pacific Cafe is a culinary delight and surprise for the small island of Kauai. Condé Nast Traveler Magazine voted this fabulous restaurant one of the top 50 restaurants in the nation! Chef–Owner, Jean–Marie Josselin creates food that is phenomenal! The flavors are extraordinary as is the presentation. The food is served on beautiful hand painted ceramic platters designed by Sophronia (Jean–Marie's wife) who was also instrumental in designing the interior of the Kauai restaurant and their new restaurant on Maui by the same name.

Jean–Marie has received many awards and has won the "National Seafood Challenge". The recipes included here were contributed from his own cookbook, "A Taste of Hawaii". Understanding that food is a "source of life", Jean–Marie has even been studying the health benefits of herbs.

The innovative menu changes daily. Examples include Seared Spicy Ahi Salad, Garlic Sesame Crust Mahi Mahi with Lime Ginger Sauce, and Chinese Roast Duck with Pineapple–Mint Sauce.

The atmosphere is busy and upbeat. Reservations are highly recommended. Dinner nightly. Entrees $13.50–$25.00.

A Pacific Cafe Maui is located in Azeka Place II Shopping Center, S. Kihei Road, Kihei (808) 879–0069.

Steamed Hawaiian Lobster Tail with Vegetables in Yellow Curry and Lime Sauce

4	Lobster Tails, each approximately ¾ pound		12	Snow Peas, cut into julienne strips
3	Ti Leaves		2	Fresh Red Chili Peppers, sliced
3 Stalks	Lemon Grass		4	Baby Japanese Eggplant, diced into ½" cubes
½ Cup	Sliced Yellow Squash, in julienne strips		2	Limes, juice only
½ Cup	Carrots, in julienne strips			
½ Cup	Zucchini, in julienne strips			

Yellow Curry and Lime Sauce

1 Cup	Sake		1 Cup	Lobster Stock
1 Teaspoon	Chopped Fresh Ginger		⅓ Cup	Heavy Cream
1 Teaspoon	Chopped Garlic		1	Lime, juice only
1 Stalk	Lemon Grass, thinly sliced		2 Teaspoons	Yellow Curry Powder

Make the sauce (yields 1 cup). In a saucepan, heat the sake, ginger, garlic, and lemon grass over high heat and reduce liquid by one third. Add stock and cream, then reduce again by one third. Add lime juice, curry powder, and simmer briefly. Set aside.

Place lobster tails in a large bamboo steamer lined with ti leaves along with lemon grass. Sprinkle with lime juice, then steam for about 4 minutes. Place vegetables in steamer along with lobster and steam another 4 minutes.

To serve, place a spoonful of the vegetables in the center of a plate; slice the steamed lobster tails in half lengthwise and place on top of steamed vegetables. Serve with the Yellow Curry and Lime Sauce. Serves four.

Sesame Tuiles with Lilikoi Sorbet

5 Tablespoons	Unsalted Butter, softened		6 Scoops	Lilikoi Sorbet
½ Teaspoon	White Sesame Seeds		3 Cups	Cut Up Fresh Fruit, such as Pineapple, Papaya, Banana, Guava, Kiwi, Raspberries, or Strawberries.
½ Teaspoon	Lime Zest			
¼ Cup	Sugar			
2	Egg Whites			
½ Cup	All-Purpose Flour			

Preheat the oven to 425 degrees F. Grease a baking sheet. In a mixing bowl, combine the butter, sesame seeds, and lime zest with a spatula. Add the sugar, egg whites, and fold in the flour. Drop batter by tablespoonfuls on the baking sheet. Flatten the batter with the rounded side of a spoon to form 6 circles about 4 inches in diameter. Bake for about 4 minutes or until the batter turns golden. With a spatula remove the cookies from the baking sheet. While still warm, gently press each over the top of a glass to form a cup. Let the tuiles cool completely before filling them with sorbet and fresh fruit. Serves six.

MEMA CUISINE

(808) 823–0899 • 4–361 Kuhio Hwy., Kapaa, Kauai 96746

Mema is a great little Thai Chinese restaurant that offers a large menu of delicious selections. The first time I ate there a friend invited me to try "this great new Thai place". She recommended the Ahi with a sweet and sour garlic sauce (it's a special, not on the menu). It was fabulous! I love their Shrimp Spring Rolls too. For those who are not familiar with the process—wrap them in the lettuce leaves with the cucumber slices and either pour on, or dip in, the delicious peanut sauce. Yum!

Mema is family owned and operated. They grow their own kaffir lime, lemon basil, and other herbs.

The owners are both second generation Chinese. William (also known as Me) came to the United States from Laos in 1978. He started out as a newspaper boy in Honolulu for 1 year, after which he began working in the restaurant business. His wife and partner Rojuna came over from Thailand in 1991.

They opened Mema in March 1992. Their philosophy was to start slow with only word of mouth for advertising and make their customers happy so they would spread the word and come back again. It works! Me explained what Mema means: "Me" means "happy, doing well, prosperous", and "ma" means "come, or you're coming". So happy prosperous people— come to Mema!

They have many vegetarian selections, flavorful curry dishes, and so much more. Many items are available mild, medium or hot, and offer a choice of chicken, beef, pork or seafood. Lunch Monday through Friday. Dinner daily. Both $6.00–$14.00. Located behind Sizzler.

Cashew Nut Chicken*

2–4 Tablespoons	Oil
½ Cup	Onion, chopped
2 Cloves	Garlic, minced
12 Ounces	Chicken, chopped, uncooked
	Salt to Taste
4 Tablespoons	Oyster Sauce

1 Cup	Roasted Cashew Nuts (deep fry raw nuts for 1–3 minutes, until they begin turning color)
	Lettuce for garnish
½ Teaspoon	Sugar
	Dried Chili (optional)

Fry a couple of tablespoons of onion in the oil, then add chicken. When cooked, add onion and garlic, then oyster sauce, sugar, salt and rest of ingredients. To make spicier, add the dried chili (chopped or whole) which has been deep fried until golden brown. Serve on a bed of lettuce. Serves two.

Mema Curry (Chicken, Shrimp or Fish)*

2 Tablespoons	Oil
2–4 Leaves	Kaffir Lime, chopped
2 Pieces	Lemon Grass, ground or finely chopped
5–8 Cloves	Garlic, chopped
2 Teaspoons	Red Curry Paste (or Yellow for milder flavor)
	Hot Chili Sauce, to taste

4 Cups	Coconut Milk
6 Tablespoons	Fish Sauce
1 Teaspoon	Sugar
12 Ounces	Chicken, raw, chopped (or Fish, or Shrimp)
3	Potatoes, cooked (by steaming), peeled, and chopped

Sauté first four ingredients together 30 seconds to 1 minute. Add red curry and hot chili sauce. Slowly stir in coconut milk. Add fish sauce and sugar, then chicken, fish or shrimp, cook only until done—just a few minutes. Then add potatoes. Serves two to three.

*Mema cooks by taste. Amounts are approximate and may need adjustments to suit your taste. Experiment and have fun! The hard to find items can be found at Asian food stores.

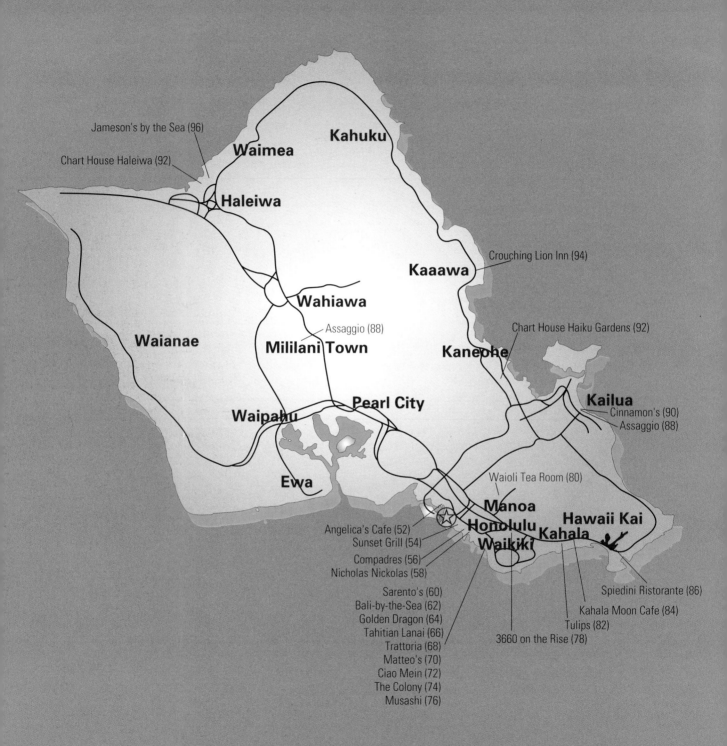

Jameson's by the Sea (96)

Chart House Haleiwa (92)

Waimea **Kahuku**

Haleiwa

Crouching Lion Inn (94)

Kaaawa

Wahiawa

Assaggio (88)

Chart House Haiku Gardens (92)

Waianae

Mililani Town **Kaneohe**

Kailua
Cinnamon's (90)
Assaggio (88)

Pearl City

Waipahu

Waioli Tea Room (80)

Ewa

Manoa
Honolulu **Hawaii Kai**
Waikiki **Kahala**

Angelica's Cafe (52)
Sunset Grill (54)

Compadres (56)
Nicholas Nickolas (58)

Spiedini Ristorante (86)

Sarento's (60)
Bali-by-the-Sea (62)
Golden Dragon (64)
Tahitian Lanai (66)
Trattoria (68)
Matteo's (70)
Ciao Mein (72)
The Colony (74)
Musashi (76)

Kahala Moon Cafe (84)

Tulips (82)

3660 on the Rise (78)

Oahu

The Gathering Place

Cuisines Featured

Angelica's Cafe was voted the "Best–Kept Dining Secret" by the readers of Honolulu Magazine. It's pleasant and small with sidewalk cafe style seating in an open air breezeway or inside where a variety of art decorates the walls. The decor is light and cheerful. Candlelight creates romance in the evenings.

Angelica's owner, Bernd Smeisser says, "I like to serve only the best or I don't serve it at all." He brings over 40 years of restaurant experience to Angelica's and works together with Executive Chef Delwyn Ondo to create an international experience. Bernd speaks 7 languages fluently!

Lunch features delicious items such as Caesar Salad with Cajun Chicken or Blackened Ahi, Roasted Eggplant Parmesan, and Gourmet Pizza Pie of the day. The dinner menu changes frequently and includes Fresh Fish, Lemon Chicken, and Roasted Rack of Baby Lamb served with a mint sauce. The desserts are mouth watering–Strawberry Napoleon, German Chocolate Cake, Raspberry Mousse, and more!

Open Monday through Saturday. Lunch $10.00–$13.00. Dinner entrées $15.00–$20.00. Reservations requested. Located between Kmart and City Mall. Free, easy parking.

Grilled Shiitake Mushrooms on Wilted Radicchio

1 Head	Radicchio	1 Teaspoon	Balsamic Vinegar
5 or 6 Large	Shiitake Mushrooms	1 Tablespoon	Grated Reggiano
½ Cup	Olive Oil		Salt and Pepper to Taste
1 Tablespoon	Blanched, Chopped Garlic		

Brush mushrooms with olive oil and grill over medium hot Kiawe wood until cooked through (turn as needed). Chop radicchio coarsely. Add to hot sauté pan with ½ tablespoon olive oil. Cook until wilted. Remove from heat, sprinkle with balsamic vinegar. Toss mushrooms with salt and pepper. Place radicchio on plate, place mushrooms on top, caps up. Garnish with reggiano.

Grilled Ahi with Tomato Basil Vinaigrette on Pasta

2	Ahi Steaks, ½" thick	2 Servings	Pasta of choice

While cooking pasta (until al dente), make vinaigrette.

Grill Ahi over charcoal until medium rare. Brush with olive oil. Put pasta on two warm plates, place Ahi on top with tomato basil mixture. May garnish with rinsed capers.

Tomato Basil Vinaigrette

2	Plum Tomatoes, diced	1 Tablespoon	White Wine Vinegar
¼ Cup	Chopped Fresh Basil	3 Tablespoons	Olive Oil
1	Shallot, finely diced		Salt and Pepper to Taste

Combine all ingredients. Set aside.

Sunset Grill is known for what Chef Doug Lum calls "New World Bistro" cuisine. His imaginative creations are American in origin but flavored with tastes from around the world. Chef Lum makes use of many local products, incorporating the tastes of Hawaii in his own distinctive way. His creativity pays off. Sunset Grill has been a Hale 'Aina (restaurant) award winner five years in a row.

Some popular creations are: Bowtie Pasta with Blackened Ahi, Kiawe grilled Fresh Fish, and the two recipes featured on the following page.

The delectable desserts including Vanilla Bean Cheesecake with Macadamia Nut Crust, and delicious Lemon Tart with fresh strawberries, are created by pastry chef, Kelli Lum (Doug's wife).

Sunset Grill offers an exciting, airy atmosphere that encourages everyone to enjoy themselves. You may doodle on the placements (crayons are provided). The best are framed and decorate the "Celebrity Wall of Fame". Or you can observe Chef Lum and his crew creating in the exhibition kitchen–it's amazing to watch.

Sunset Grill participates in Green Cuisine, a movement which promotes awareness and support for food grown with little or no chemicals. Being health conscious is part of the philosophy at Sunset Grill (they also recycle) and everything is fresh–no preservatives or stabilizers are used.

Open daily. Lunch $9.00–$18.00. Sunday brunch. Dinner entrées $9.00–$24.00. Validated parking in the Restaurant Row garage.

Smoked Infused Marinated Salmon with Oriental Shiitake Mushroom Salsa

3 Pounds	Norwegian Salmon

Ginger Vinaigrette

2 Cups	Shoyu		½ Cup	Sugar
½ Cup	Rice Wine Vinegar		4 Ounces	Ginger

Mix shoyu, vinegar and sugar. Smash ginger with mortar and pestle (or hammer), add to other ingredients. Let sit for 10 minutes.

Cut the salmon into individual servings and marinate for 30 minutes in 6 ounces of the ginger vinaigrette. Smoke using apple wood for 2½ minutes. Set aside to grill later. Meanwhile prepare the salsa.

Oriental Shiitake Mushroom Salsa

8 Ounces	Ginger Vinaigrette		6 Each	Roma Tomatoes, small, diced
1 Pound	Fresh Shiitake Mushrooms			
2 Medium	Red Onions, finely diced		1 Bunch	Green Onions
1 Bunch	Chopped Cilantro		To Taste	Sherry
2 Tablespoons	Toasted Sesame Seeds			

Lightly sauté the shiitakes in olive oil. Add the onions and cook for one minute, add sherry. Reduce. Add 2 ounces of ginger vinaigrette and remove from heat. Mix in tomatoes, cilantro, green onions and sesame seeds. Grill salmon and top with salsa. Serve with sautéed vegetables.

Chicken–Gorgonzola Salad

6 Ounces	Boneless, Skinless Chicken Breasts		2 Ounces	Walnuts, unsalted
			1	Granny Smith Apple
2 Ounces	Gorgonzola Cheese		2 Ounces	Balsamic Vinaigrette

Grill chicken breast just before serving to insure that it is moist, tender, and warm. Place mixed baby lettuces onto an entrée sized serving plate, sprinkle half of the nuts and cheese atop the greens, slice the chicken on an extreme bias and arrange in a fan atop the salad. Next, core the apple and slice in half from stem to end. Place cut side down on a cutting board and slice thinly. Using four slices each, make four apple fans and arrange around the border of the salad. Drizzle with equal parts of aged balsamic vinegar and extra virgin olive oil, or use your favorite vinaigrette. Serves one.

Compadres was recommended by many people for its fabulous food and fun atmosphere. In the evenings you can almost always find something going on: live music, or theme parties focusing on an event that is happening in the community (such as a surf or film festival party). The food is fresh and features "Western cooking with a Mexican accent." Compadres was voted "Best Mexican Restaurant" and "One of the Top 20 Restaurants in Hawaii", by the readers of Honolulu Magazine.

Compadres was founded by Rick Enos and Dick Bradley in 1984 at the Ward Centre location. There are also locations in Northern California and one on Maui, at the Lahaina Cannery Mall. Travel/Holiday Magazine wrote, "At Compadres the emphasis is on the pleasure of eating." You can enjoy items such as the Quesadillas Internacionales–each choice of quesadilla features a different flavor from around the world. The Tamal de la Casa is filled with different ingredients each day (also offered vegetarian). Even their Casa Relleno is offered with a choice of filling (chorizo, chicken, beef or seafood). Other specialties include Chile Colorado and Al Carbon Fajitas. The children's menu is great and fun for the kids! For dessert try an Apple Chimichanga or Caramel Flan. The Margaritas are well praised, as is their wine list.

Look for the great murals on the walls painted by Honolulu artist, Peggy Chun.

Lunch and dinner $7.00–$17.00. Open daily.

Tamal de la Casa

1 Package	Frozen Banana Leaves, thawed and cut into six 15–20" pieces		½ Teaspoon	White Pepper
				Salt to Taste
2 Pounds	Masa (corn dough, found in Mexican grocery stores)		½ Cup	Water
			2 Pounds	Salmon
5 Ounces	Butter or Vegetable Lard		3 Cups	Each of Cooked Black Beans/Corn
½ Teaspoon	Baking Powder		1 Bunch	Dill

In a large bowl, mix masa, butter, baking powder, white pepper, salt and water. For each tamal, place one of the banana leaves on a work surface, spread masa and put in 5 ounces salmon, ½ cup black beans, ½ cup corn, and dill. Fold the banana leaf at the bottom over the filling. Continue folding the leaf around the filling until you reach the opposite end of the leaf. Fold in the sides of the leaf like a letter to form a rectangular packet. Steam tamales for 45 minutes. To serve, open the packet and serve tamales in their wrappers. Serves six.

Tortilla Soup

1 Large	Chicken		Oil for deep frying
½	Onion, chopped		Grated Provolone or Mozzarella Cheese
2 Stalks	Celery, chopped		
1	Bay Leaf		Chopped Cilantro
	Peppercorns		Salsa Fresca (recipe
	Corn Tortillas		below)

Salsa Fresca

2 Large	Tomatoes		Chopped Cilantro
1	Avocado	½	Lime, juice only
6	Green Onions		Salt to Taste
2	Serrano Chiles		

Dice, peel, and seed tomatoes and avocado. Chop green onions, including the tops. Seed and chop serrano chiles. Mix all ingredients with a wooden spoon.

Mix first five soup ingredients in a large stock pot. Add water to cover and bring to a boil. Reduce heat and simmer for 45 minutes to 1 hour, depending on the size of the chicken. Allow chicken to cool in the liquid. When chicken is cool, remove skin and bones and shred meat. Strain stock through cheesecloth. Cut tortillas into long strips, then fry in hot oil until crisp. For each serving place ½ cup shredded chicken in an oven proof soup bowl. Pour in chicken stock. Add several crisp tortilla chips. Sprinkle with grated cheese. Place in oven under broiler unit until cheese melts. Sprinkle with chopped cilantro and top with a tablespoon of Salsa Fresca. Serves six.

For Chicken or Beef Fajita Salad with Avocado Vinaigrette from Compadres see page 183. (Requested by *Bon Appetit* Magazine.)

NICHOLAS NICKOLAS THE RESTAURANT

(808) 955-4466 • 410 Atkinson Dr., Ala Moana Hotel, Honolulu, HI 96814

I arrived in time to see the sun setting over the ocean, with the last of the evening glow, while the city lights came to life. Nicholas Nickolas, located on the 36th floor of the Ala Moana Hotel, offers a spectacular panoramic view of Waikiki, Diamond Head and the Pacific Ocean.

Owned by partners Nick Nickolas and Jeff Harmon, with managing partners Steve Karpf and Aaron Placourakis, Nicholas Nickolas has been providing outstanding food and excellent service since 1985. Harmon and Nickolas have spent many years perfecting their approach to fine dining since forming their partnership in 1965. They now own several restaurants from Hawaii to Florida.

One of their secrets to success is that everyone starts out as a dishwasher or busboy, and is promoted by performance and attitude, not seniority. This approach helps keep the quality and consistency of the food and service high. The wait staff is very knowledgeable, friendly, and accommodating. Their descriptions of food are mouth-watering.

The Black and Blue Ahi, served with a mustard sauce is outstanding as an appetizer. Recommended entrées include Blackened Onaga, Opaka Katina, and Porterhouse Steak broiled over kiawe wood. They feature an extensive wine list and many tantalizing desserts: fresh strawberries served with brown sugar and devonshire cream for dipping, a subtle Mocha Mousse, and many more.

Live music and dancing can be enjoyed nightly. Valet parking. Call for reservations. Dinner nightly. Entrees $18.00-$43.00.

Maryland Crab Cakes with Lemon Garlic Chili Sauce

3	16 Ounce Cans Lump Maryland Blue Crab Meat	¾ Teaspoon	Colemans Mustard
1 Small	Red Bell Pepper	3	Eggs
1 Small	Green Bell Pepper	½ Cup	Bread Crumbs
1 Small	Yellow Bell Pepper	⅓ Cup	Mayonnaise

Dice red, green, and yellow bell peppers, set aside. Sift through crab meat to ensure cartilage and shells are removed. In a mixing bowl add all ingredients except bread crumbs. Mix thoroughly. Add bread crumbs, less for a looser batch, more for a tighter batch. In a sauté pan over medium–high heat, sauté until golden–brown on both sides. Serve on a bed of Lemon Garlic Chili Sauce (recipe below). Serves four to six.

Lemon Garlic Chili Sauce

3 Ounces	White Wine	½ Teaspoon	Minced Garlic
1 Teaspoon	Red Pepper Puree	½ Teaspoon	Chopped Chili Pepper
1 Ounce	Lemon Juice	3 Ounces	Butter
1 Teaspoon	Chopped Fresh Basil		

In a sauté pan, over high heat, add all the ingredients, cooking to a simmer then reduce heat and whip in 3 ounces butter.

Mahi Ala Lexi

2	Mahi Fillets lightly rubbed with Olive Oil

Herbal Bread Crumbs

2 Cups	Panko Bread Crumbs (Japanese)	1 Teaspoon	Tarragon
1 Teaspoon	Oregano	1 Tablespoon	Paprika
1 Teaspoon	Basil	2 Ounces	Sherry
		3 Ounces	Drawn Butter

In a mixing bowl, add all ingredients and mix thoroughly.

Lobster Veloute

2 Quarts	Lobster Stock (lobster base can be substituted)	1 Teaspoon	Thyme
1 Teaspoon	Oregano	1 Cup	Heavy Whipping Cream
1 Teaspoon	Basil	3 Ounces	Butter

In a sauce pan, add all ingredients, reduce stock by ½. Reduce heat. Enrich stock by whipping in cream and butter. Simmer for 2–3 minutes.

After rubbing mahi with olive oil, spread herbal bread crumb mixture over top of fillets and bake in the oven at 350 degrees for 7–10 minutes. Remove, top with Lobster Veloute, and serve. Serves two.

The wonderful experience of Sarento's begins with a ride in the glass elevator that takes you up to the 29th floor of the Ilikai Hotel. Once there, you step into the beautiful and elegant decor of Sarento's, with expansive views including Diamond Head, the Pacific Ocean, and Honolulu. Opened in 1994, Sarento's is owned by the same partners that own Nicholas Nickolas. The influence of managing partner Aaron Placourakis is felt. Sarento's is named after his grandfather. Aaron says, "He was a simple, unpretentious family man. Sarento's was created in his honor–a place where you feel comfortable breaking bread." In the dining room there is a large mural of the partners with family and friends "breaking bread". The mural and a wood burning pizza oven in full view, add a warmth and comfortableness to the room. Individual rooms are available for a quieter, more private setting, as well as intimate booths. Almost every table features an outstanding view. Aaron says, "Sarento's is not one–dimensional. The view is the icing on the cake, not the sole reason for coming."

Their signature dish is Filet Nicolini–gorgonzola melted over filet of beef with walnuts, fried leeks and a cabernet sauce. Sarento's French Canadian Chef Dan Chevalier created Swordfish Daniello–fresh swordfish coated with herbs, sautéed, and served with pomodora sauce. The knowledgeable and gracious staff at Sarento's can help you choose the right wine from their vast selection to enhance your dinner. The desserts are intriguing and unique, including Sarento's signature dessert–banana pizza!

Call for reservations. Valet parking. Dinner nightly. Entrees $15.00–$36.00.

Seafood Fra Diavlo

1	Lobster Tail (remove from shell and dice into 1" pieces)	1 Large Pinch	Crushed Red Pepper
		6 Med/Large	Shrimp
		6	Blue Gold Mussels
2 Ounces	White Wine	4 Ounces	Olive Oil
8 Ounces	Linguine	4 Ounces	Chopped Basil
12 Ounces	Marinara Sauce (see recipe below)	4 Ounces	Garlic Butter (see recipe below)

Sauté all seafood in olive oil. Add white wine, red pepper, fresh basil, then reduce. Add marinara and garlic butter. Simmer 3–5 minutes. Toss with cooked linguine and serve. Serves two.

Marinara Sauce

¼ Cup	Olive Oil	1 Tablespoon	Thyme
1 Large	Diced Onion	1 Tablespoon	Basil
¼ Cup	Minced Garlic	½ Teaspoon	Red Pepper
3	15 Ounce Cans Plum Tomatoes, hand squeezed	½ Teaspoon	Black Pepper
8 Ounce Can	Tomato Paste	1 Ounce	Salt
1 Cup	Red Wine	1 Ounce	Sugar
3 Tablespoons	Oregano	2 Teaspoons	Rosemary
		2	Bay Leaves

Sauté onions in olive oil. Add spices, wine, garlic, tomatoes and paste. Simmer ½ hour. Yield: one gallon of sauce. Sauce can be stored up to one month in refrigerator.

Garlic Butter

2 Pounds	Butter, softened	Dash	Tabasco
1 Tablespoon	Garlic Powder	2 Tablespoons	White Wine
1 Tablespoon	Minced Fresh Garlic	1 Teaspoon	Brandy
½ Teaspoon	Worcestershire Sauce	2 Tablespoons	Chopped Parsley
½ Teaspoon	Bitters		

Place butter in mixer. Add all dry ingredients, blend. Add all liquids, blend.

For Key Lime Tarts from Sarento's, see page 184.

I arrived early for breakfast and sat comfortably in the casually elegant surroundings of Bali–by–the–Sea. The ocean breeze blew by as I enjoyed the incredibly beautiful morning. Waikiki Beach was quiet with long shadows. I watched people taking off on a boat expedition. What a wonderful place to enjoy breakfast, lunch, and a romantic sunset dinner!

Breakfast menu selections include fresh fish, omelets, French toast, waffles with fresh strawberries, and more. For lunch they serve Pot Stickers with roast pepper pesto, salads and sandwiches, and entrées such as Roast Chicken with fettucine, shiitake mushrooms and asparagus, or Salmon baked in rice paper served with a mandarin citrus dressing. For dinner, along with a regular menu, they feature a Chef's menu that changes every few days offering a selection of appetizers, soup or salad, entrées (Brochette of Scallops and Shrimps with julienne of carrots and leeks with ginger sauce or Breast of Duck with black currants and oranges...) and a choice of luscious desserts, and coffee, all for $37.50.

Chef Jean–Luc Voegele takes pride in his culinary works, using local ingredients and creating exquisite presentations. Originally from France, he has worked in Hong Kong and, brings experience from the famous Michelin Star Restaurants.

Breakfast $5.00–$15.50. Lunch $10.00–$19.00. Both served Monday through Friday. Dinner nightly. Entrees $25.00–$28.50. Jackets optional. Reservations recommended. Complimentary valet parking at the Rainbow Tower.

Grilled Eggplant Lasagna with Basil Beurre Blanc

18 Slices	Large Round Eggplant cut ½" thick		1 Ounce	Red Bell Pepper
	Salt and Pepper		1 Ounce	Yellow Bell Pepper
2 Ounces	Cherry Tomatoes		1 Ounce	Onions, chopped
2 Ounces	Tofu		1 Teaspoon	Garlic, chopped
2 Ounces	Green Zucchini		½ Teaspoon	Thyme
2 Ounces	Yellow Squash, cut in small pieces		½ Cup	Olive Oil
				Salt and Pepper
				Basil Leaves for garnish

Basil Beurre Blanc

1 Ounce	Shallots, chopped			Salt and Pepper
½ Cup	White Wine		½	Lemon, juice only
½ Cup	Fresh Cream			Fresh Chopped Basil
2 Ounces	Butter			

Reduce white wine and shallots ¾; add cream, reduce by half. Whisk in butter, add chopped basil, lemon juice, salt and pepper.

For Ratatouille, sauté all vegetables in olive oil. Season with salt and pepper.

Brush the eggplant with oil, season with salt and pepper, and grill. Alternate layers of eggplant, Ratatouille, and Beurre Blanc.

Sautéed Opakapaka on Stir Fried Vegetables, Ginger and Watercress Couli

20 Ounces	Opakapaka Fillet		1 Teaspoon	Oil
	Olive Oil		9 Teaspoons	Soy Sauce
	Salt and Pepper		1 Teaspoon	Oyster Sauce
4 Ounces	Bok Choy		1 Teaspoon	Chili Sauce
3 Ounces	Choy Sum		¼ Teaspoon	Sesame Oil
3 Ounces	Bean Sprouts		1 Ounce	Ginger, julienne
2 Ounces	Red Bell Peppers		4 Ounces	Wild Rice

Watercress Couli

½ Cup	White Wine		2 Ounces	Butter
1 Ounce	Shallots		1 Bunch	Watercress
2 Ounces	Cream			

Reduce white wine and shallots by ¾; add cream and reduce by half. Whip with fresh butter and blanched chopped watercress. Season with salt, pepper, and lemon juice.

Sauté the Opakapaka in a pan. Stir fry all the vegetables in a wok and add all the seasoning and spices. Deep fry the ginger for garnish.

The Golden Dragon has won many awards, including "Hawaii's Best Restaurant" and "Best Chinese Cuisine", and it is listed as one of Hawaii's top twenty restaurants. A very unique thing about the Golden Dragon are the lovely tea ladies who visit your table to serve exotic Chinese teas, explain some background about the tea, and tell your Chinese horoscope. I found out that I was born in the year of the Ox —a symbol of prosperity. "Ox people are calm, quiet but sometimes eccentric and dogmatic..."?! It's fascinating. My tea lady told me that some people get so wrapped up in their horoscope that they need to be reminded that it's for entertainment purposes only. It is fun. And so is the restaurant's menu. They feature an extensive variety of appetizing dishes. Chef Steve Chiang's signature selection includes seven delicious courses: Seafood and vegetable egg rolls, crispy won tons, island pork char siu, hot and sour soup, stir fried chicken with eggplant in garlic sauce, wok seared scallops and beef with vegetables, lovers of lobster and shrimp, pepper and duck fried rice, and lychee ice cream.

They offer three other full course dinners and over 50 dishes available ala carte. An intriguing dish I would like to try next time, is the Imperial Beggar's Chicken which is wrapped in lotus leaves and encased in clay before it is baked (this requires a 24 hour notice and serves two).

Dining at Golden Dragon is a wonderful experience that you can enjoy indoors or on their large lanai overlooking a peaceful lagoon. Jackets are optional. Reservations recommended. Dinner Tuesday through Sunday. Entrees $11.00–$30.00. Full course dinners $28.00–$47.00. Complimentary valet parking at the Rainbow Tower.

Kung Pao Chicken

2 Tablespoons	Hoisin Sauce		1	Egg White
1 Tablespoon	Ketchup		1 Teaspoon	Cornstarch
1 Tablespoon	Soy Sauce			Finely Chopped Green
2 Teaspoons	Vinegar			Onion
2 Teaspoons	Sugar		8 Pieces	Small Dried Red Pepper
2 Teaspoons	Brandy		5 Tablespoons	Vegetable Oil
1 Teaspoon	Sesame Oil		2 Ounces	Deep Fried Rice Sticks
6 Ounces	Deboned Chicken			

Mix together Hoisin sauce, ketchup, soy sauce, vinegar, sugar, brandy and sesame oil, set aside. Marinate chicken with egg white, cornstarch and half of vegetable oil. Turn wok or frying pan on high and add the balance of vegetable oil. Deep fry rice noodles at high heat for 3–5 seconds, until they expand into large rice sticks and set aside on paper towels to absorb excess oil. Drop chicken into hot wok or frying pan, for approximately 45 seconds until meat turns pinkish gray. Take out chicken and put aside. Put dry chili peppers into the wok or pan and sauté until peppers turn black. Add chopped onion and Hoisin sauce mixture. Add precooked chicken to pan and stir–fry at high heat for 15 seconds. Place rice sticks on plate and pour Kung Pao chicken over bed of rice sticks. If you desire, garnish with tomato rose and mint leaf. You may substitute with a bed of white steamed rice in place of rice sticks. Serves two.

Hong Kong Fried Rice

2 Cups	Steamed Rice		1 Tablespoon	Soy Sauce
2 Ounces	Diced Char Siu (Marinated		1 Touch	Pepper and Sugar
	Sweet Pork)		1 Teaspoon	Sesame Seed Oil
1 Ounce	Chopped Green Onion		1 Tablespoon	Salad Oil
1	Egg			

Scramble and cook egg, slice into 1" strips. Sauté the char siu in salad oil. Mix the soy sauce, pepper, sugar, and sesame seed oil in a bowl. Pour steamed rice into wok or frying pan. Pour the mixture of soy sauce, pepper, sugar, and sesame seed oil and strips of scrambled egg over rice and stir. Garnish with chopped green onion (optional). Serves two.

TAHITIAN LANAI

(808) 946–6541 • 1811 Ala Moana Blvd., Waikiki, Honolulu, Oahu 96815

Tahitian Lanai has been a favorite of residents and visitors alike for many years. You can enjoy the historical, charming Polynesian atmosphere from early in the morning, until the wee hours after midnight (7:00 a.m.–2:00 a.m.). It's very pleasant to sit by the pool, or enjoy the privacy offered by the individual thatched roof huts—each named after Tahitian Royalty.

My brother, who lives in California, loves the Tahitian Lanai and recommends it to all his friends who come to Oahu, who also go home with great reviews. The setting is so perfectly representative of Hawaii that "Magnum P.I." and "Hawaii Five–O" have filmed scenes there.

Tahitian Lanai is known for having great Eggs Benedict. They also serve waffles, pancakes, omelets, Portuguese sausage and fried taro for breakfast. For lunch they offer a variety of salads, sandwiches, chicken or shrimp curry and teriyaki steak. Dinners feature a nice selection of fresh fish and other seafood specialties, steaks, chicken and ribs. Tahitian Lanai is the only restaurant in Hawaii that is approved by Heart Smart Restaurants International®, and offers tasty items that are low in fat, sodium and cholesterol, with nutritional information available to help health conscious guests make better choices.

For some entertaining fun check out the Hawaiian sing–a–long (nightly) at the Papeete Bar. Some of the regulars have been joining in for over 30 years!

Complimentary valet parking available. Open daily. Breakfast and lunch under $11.00. Dinner $15.00–$30.00.

Seafood Marinara

2 Pieces	Shrimp			Olive Oil
1½ Ounces	Mahimahi		2 Ounces	Parmesan Cheese
3 Pieces	Scallops		6 Ounces	Pasta Noodles (Fettucine,
3 Ounces	King Crab			Linguine or Rotelle)
4 Pieces	Clams		8 Ounces	Marinara Sauce

Sauté seafood in olive oil. Just before seafood is cooked, add ½ cup of the marinara sauce and continue to sauté until seafood is finished. Toss with cooked pasta and top with parmesan cheese. Serves two.

Marinara Sauce

1 Cup	Olive Oil		½ Tablespoon	Black Pepper
1	Diced Onion		1¾ Tablespoons	Oregano Leaves
1 Tablespoon	Fresh Garlic, minced		2	Bay Leaves

Sauté the above ingredients. Mix the following ingredients with the above sautéed ingredients.

3 Pounds	Diced Tomatoes, fresh or canned		12 Ounces	Tomato Paste, canned
			½ Gallon	Water
1½ Pounds	Tomato Sauce, canned		4 Ounces	Chicken Base

Cook for 1 hour on low heat. Serves approximately 6 people. Sauce may be frozen.

E'ia Ota—Tahitian Marinated Sashimi for Two

8 Ounces	Fresh Sashimi		1	Fresh Lime, juiced
1	Fresh Lemon, juiced			

Marinate fresh fish in lime and lemon juice over night. Wash in cold water the next day.

8 Ounces	Coconut Milk		2 Ounces	Cucumber, diced
2 Ounces	Fresh Tomatoes, diced		2 Ounces	Onion, diced

Mix ingredients, toss with fresh fish and serve.

TRATTORIA ITALIAN RESTAURANT
(808) 923-8415 • 2168 Kalia Road, Waikiki, Honolulu, Oahu 96815

I had heard Trattoria was festive and fun. When I walked in I did notice the festive feeling and ambiance. It is casual, unpretentious, and fun, with incredible aromas filling the air as some food gets the final touches of preparation at your table. The hand painted frescos on the walls create a nice authentic touch to go with the Northern Italian cuisine.

Trattoria features fabulous seafood, veal, chicken, and beef selections. For example—Mahi Mahi alla Veronica, sautéed island fish served with lemon sauce and seedless grapes or Scampi (prawns) alla Trattoria and Piccata di Vitello, thin slices of milk-fed veal sautéed with lemon butter and a white wine caper sauce. Other choices include the homemade Tortellini filled with mortadella, chicken, spices and served with white cheese sauce, tomato or meat sauce, and of course, a great selection of other pastas, and more! To top off your festive dining experience, try the Crepes Trattoria for dessert—custard filled crepes flambéed at the table and served with strawberry sauce, laced with Kirsch and Triple Sec. It's decadent, especially with the Cappuccino alla Trattoria!

Valet parking available. Reservations recommended. Dinner nightly. Entrees $10.00–$27.00. Dinners $18.00–$24.00.

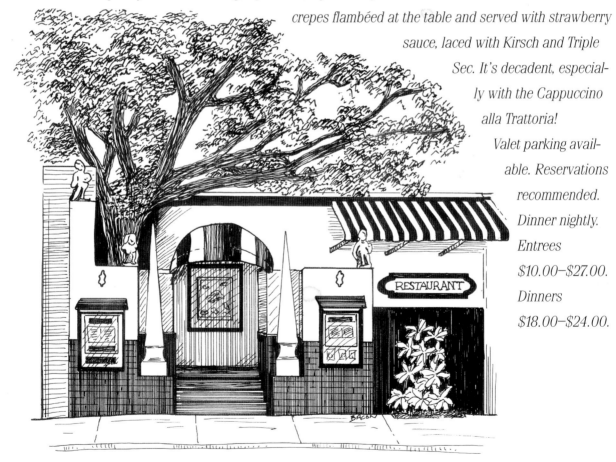

Chicken Primavera

6 Ounces	Julienne Carrots			Dry Basil
6 Ounces	Julienne Zucchini			Red Pepper
6 Medium	Mushrooms, cut into thirds			Grated Parmesan Cheese
1 Tablespoon	Chopped Garlic		6 Ounces	Uncooked Pasta
⅓ Cup	Extra Virgin Olive Oil		6 Ounces	Julienne Cut Chicken Thighs
	Salt		4	Fresh Basil Leaves
	Pepper			

Place carrots, zucchini, mushrooms and chicken into sauce pan with olive oil. Season to taste with salt, pepper, basil and red pepper. Sauté over high heat about 1½ minutes. Be careful not to burn the oil. Place ingredients into a 450 degree oven for 5 minutes, occasionally mixing ingredients to keep the cooking even. Meanwhile cook pasta in boiling water with oil and salt. When pasta is cooked, drain and place in a bowl. Add 1 tablespoon of olive oil, pinch of dry basil and 1 tablespoon of parmesan cheese. Mix well and cover. When chicken and vegetable mixture is done, mix into bowl with pasta. Toss together and serve. Serves one.

Calamari Salad

25 Ounces	¼" Cut, Cleaned Squid		5 Dashes	Tabasco
2 Cups	Olive Oil		½ Cup	Finely Chopped Onions
1 Tablespoon	Chopped Garlic		1	Diced Tomato
½ Tablespoon	Chopped Shallots		¼ Cup	Red Wine Vinegar
¼ Cup	Chopped Green Onions			Salt
1 Teaspoon	Lemon Juice			Pepper

Blanch squid 45 seconds in boiling water. Drain and immediately cool with ice cold water. Drain again and mix with all remaining ingredients. Let stand for 3 hours covered in the refrigerator. Serve tossed over green salad. Serves eight.

Matteo's has the honor of being voted "Hawaii's Most Popular Italian Restaurant" by the readers of Honolulu Magazine for 11 years in a row! They also won "Best Italian Cuisine" in 1994. They obviously know how to make their customers happy. While you are enjoying a romantic dinner in one of their cozy, intimate booths, when it's your birthday, you can have a complimentary photograph taken. It is usually developed by the time you finish dinner so you can take it home with you as a memory of the evening.

The executive chef, Andy Nelson, considers his style of cuisine "contemporary—which takes influences from around the Pacific Rim, Europe and the American Southwest." He was a first place winner in both the "Hawaii Seafood Competition", and the "Trya Papaya Hall of Fame" (I love that name).

Matteo's features great appetizers including Spicy Clams Italiano and special Bruschettas prepared daily by the chef. They offer Seafood Lasagna, Breast of Chicken alla Matteo's served with Spinach Pancetta, and many fresh fish, veal, beef and pork selections. Their wine list is the winner of Wine Spectator Magazine's "Best of the Award of Excellence". And for dessert, try a creation by pastry chef, Patrice Masters—Tira Misu in a chocolate tulip cup or Creme Brulee with fresh fruit.

Dinner nightly. Entrees $15.00–$30.00. Complete dinners from selected entrées $24.45–$33.45. Call for reservations. Valet parking is available from Kuhio Avenue.

Grilled Island Opakapaka with Cumin Seed Beurre Blanc and Fire Roasted Red Pepper Pesto

4	3 Ounce Fillets Fresh Hawaiian Red Snapper
½ Teaspoon	Garlic, finely chopped
¾ Teaspoon	Shallots, finely chopped
½ Teaspoon	Italian Parsley, chopped
1¼ Teaspoon	Lime Juice
1 Teaspoon	Fresh Sweet Basil, chopped
To Taste	Kosher Salt
4 Ounces	Extra Virgin Olive Oil
8 Ounces	Linguini

Combine all ingredients together and mix well. Add fish fillets and marinate in mixture for approximately 1½ hours. Cook linguini al dente. Remove fish and grill over moderate heat to desired doneness. Slightly undercooking the fish is recommended to insure moistness.

Serve fish on a bed of linguini pasta in the center of the plate. Pour cumin seed Beurre Blanc (recipe below) around fish. Pour pesto (recipe below) into a squirt bottle and drizzle over sauce. Garnish fish with a basil sprig. Serves two as an entrée.

Cumin Seed Beurre Blanc

½ Ounce	Shallots, chopped
½ Ounce	White Wine Vinegar
2 Ounces	Chardonnay Wine
½ Ounce	Cumin Seeds (toasted)
Pinch	Italian Saffron
6 Ounces	Heavy Cream
10 Ounces	Sweet Butter

Sauté shallots lightly in a little butter. Add wine, vinegar, and saffron. Simmer slowly. Remove from heat and incorporate butter chips, stirring constantly. Strain and add toasted cumin seeds. Check and adjust to desired taste.

Fire Roasted Red Pepper Pesto

⅓ Cup	Sweet Basil
⅓ Cup	Italian Parsley
4 Tablespoons	Extra Virgin Olive Oil
1 Tablespoon	Capers
To Taste	Kosher Salt
¾ Tablespoon	Parmegiano Regiano Cheese, freshly grated
1	Red Bell Pepper, fire roasted over an open flame, peeled and seeded

Combine all ingredients except red peppers into a food processor and blend. Add roasted peppers and process until it reaches a smooth consistency.

For Spicy Steamed Clams Italiano from Matteo's, see page 184.

Ciao Mein is eclectic, fun, and interesting, not to mention avant garde. Italian and Chinese seems like an odd combination of cuisines—yet this is the concept at Ciao Mein, and it is incredibly popular! Starting with a unique concept, they have continued to play up on the theme of being creative and different, like the way the table settings are at an angle and the way the water is served. It's fun to notice these things. Ciao Mein loves special occasions and even seems to create them in their festive atmosphere. Semi–private rooms are available, each with a different ambiance. One room even has a large wall of water falling down over a glass pane as a focal point.

Ciao Mein serves fabulous food and won in several categories at the "Taste of Honolulu" exhibition, including "Best Desserts" (for their Tiramisu), "Best Vegetarian", and "Most Exotic". They offer a predominately Italian wine list (the entertaining wait staff will be happy to guide you in your selection), wonderful breads like basil and sun dried tomato, and a very creative assortment of items on the menu, which are all served family style. The Szechwan Eggplant is their award winning appetizer. Whole steamed fish is truly sensational, flavorful and moist, or try Honey Walnut Shrimp, or Stir Fried Chicken and Lobster with vegetables on a bed of crispy cake noodle.

Complimentary valet parking is available. Dinner nightly. Entrees $10.00–$20.00. Sunday brunch. Call for reservations.

Steamed Whole Fish

1	Whole Fish, 1–1¼ Pound, Stripe Bass, Opakapaka, Mullet, etc., scaled, and cleaned	1 Ounce	Chinese Parsley, cut 1½" long
3–4 Pieces	Green Onion, 4—5" long	6 Ounces	Soy Sauce Mixture (3 Ounces Soy Sauce, 2 Ounces Water, ½ Ounce Sugar, mixed)
2 Ounces	Ginger, peeled and cut into fine julienne	4 Ounces	Very Hot Oil
1 Teaspoon	Sesame Seed Oil		

Place green onions on a platter. Lay whole fish on the green onion, steam for 15–18 minutes. Place julienne vegetables on top of steamed fish and splash 1 teaspoon sesame oil on top of fish. Pour 4 ounces of very hot oil evenly over the fish. Pour soy sauce mixture on top of fish. Garnish with Chinese parsley and serve hot.

Szechwan Eggplant

Mother Sauce

1½ Pounds	Koon Chun Sauce Factory Bean Sauce	⅓ Cup	Tuong Ot Toi Vietnam Chili Garlic Sauce
2 Cups	Water	⅓ Cup	Ketchup
1 Cup	Rice Vinegar	⅓ Cup	Sesame Seed Oil
1 Cup	Sugar (Granulated)		

Mix well. Can keep in refrigerator for three weeks.

10 Ounces	Chinese Long Eggplant (peeled and cut into 3" long pieces and then cut into quarters)	1 Ounce	Chicken Broth
		2–3 Slices	Fresh Red Chili Peppers
		4 Ounces	Mother Sauce
1 Tablespoon	Salad Oil	Sprig	Chinese Parsley
½ Teaspoon	Chopped Garlic	1 Teaspoon	Cornstarch dissolved in 2 teaspoons of water to thicken
½ Teaspoon	Chopped Ginger		
1 Tablespoon	Sherry Wine		

Deep fry eggplant for 1½—2 minutes. Heat salad oil in wok. Add ginger, garlic and eggplant. Stir fry. Add sherry wine, chicken broth and Mother Sauce. Adjust thickness of sauce with the dissolved cornstarch. Transfer to plate and garnish with Chinese parsley.

THE COLONY

(808) 923–1234 • Hyatt Regency Waikiki, 2424 Kalakaua Ave., Honolulu, Oahu 9681

The Colony is a comfortable and relaxed place to enjoy great steak and seafood. Old Hawaiian prints framed in Koa wood accent the walls, and soft jazz plays in the background. The atmosphere created by the staff is friendly, fun, and good spirited.

They feature an outstanding salad bar with extensive selections to choose from including many unique items such as Grilled Chicken with Peanut Sauce, Marinated Peppers, and Seasoned Grilled Eggplant. But don't fill up too much at the salad bar, because their other food is also excellent. For an appetizer I tried the incredible Blackened Ahi with pineapple relish, and for dinner the equally delicious Seafood Brochette—scallops, prawns, and vegetables on a bed of saffron rice (recipes on next page). Other dinner choices include: lobster, fresh fish, and a wide variety of steaks (you can choose the cut and size to your liking). And, for the grand finale of your dinner, they feature a dessert bar called the "Outrageous Dessert Oasis" with tempting cakes, pies, mousses, flan and fresh fruits.

For children under 12 smaller portions are available at half price. Located on the second floor of the Diamond Head Tower. Complimentary valet parking available.

Dinner nightly. $16.00–$43.00.

74

Blackened Ahi with Pineapple Relish

2 Pieces	Ahi Block 4" X 2" X 3/4"	Cajun Spice
1 Ounce	Salad Oil	

Season ahi with Cajun Spice and sear in very hot iron skillet on both sides. Slice ahi neatly and serve with relish.

Relish

1 Cup	Chopped Pineapple	½ Teaspoon	Jalapeño Pepper, minced
1 Teaspoon	Minced Garlic	2 Teaspoons	Finely Chopped Chinese Parsley
2 Teaspoons	Finely Chopped Red Bell Pepper		Salt to Taste

Combine above ingredients and mix well. Serve with Ahi.

Seafood Brochette

10	Large Shrimp with tail on, peeled and deveined	Salt and Pepper for Seasoning
10	Large Scallops	Oil
2	10" Long Metal Skewers	

Place scallop inside of shrimp, and skewer (5 pieces each). Brush lightly with oil, season with salt and pepper, and cook under broiler until done.

Sauce

2 Ounces	Chopped Garlic	1 Cup	White Wine
2 Ounces	Chopped Shallots	2 Cups	Heavy Cream
2 Slices	Bay Leaves	½ Pound	Softened Butter
1 Teaspoon	White Peppercorn	½	Lemon, juice only

Combine first five ingredients in a sauce pot, simmer and reduce to ¼ of original amount. Add heavy cream and reduce again to ⅓. Blend in softened butter a little at a time, using wire whisk. Adjust seasoning and add lemon juice. Strain with china cap or cheese cloth. Place seafood skewer on plate, pour sauce over. Garnish with rice pilaf or saffron rice and desired vegetables. Serves two.

I was delighted and amazed at the plate presented to me at Musashi. It contained many compartments— each filled with something delicious. Some were interesting and unique to me, and very tasty. Others were familiar, including delicious morsels of shrimp, duck and salmon. What a delightful dining experience! I had the good fortune of meeting Ricky Oshima, the executive sous chef for Musashi, The Colony and Ciao Mein. He pleasantly answered all my curious questions about the delicacies that I was enjoying so much.

Musashi also features a Sushi Bar, Shabu Shabu, and a Teppan–Yaki grille, where your dinner is prepared right before your eyes. It's fun and entertaining. Dinner selections include: Lobster, Shrimp Tempura, Filet Mignon, Sashimi, Sukiyaki, and many more! Dinners are served with miso soup, steamed rice, pickled vegetables, green tea, and some also include salad, shrimps and stir fried vegetables. For dessert try some refreshing green tea sherbet or ice cream tempura with strawberry coulis.

The restaurant looks out into a lovely garden. Breakfast is served starting at 5:30 a.m. for early risers. Four full breakfasts are offered—two are traditional Japanese and two feature American food.

Open daily. Breakfast $16.00. Full dinners $22.00–$44.00.

Aigamo No Kuwayaki (Tender Duck Breast with Special Sauce)

8 Ounces	Thinly Sliced Duck Breast, 1 ounce each, 8 slices	2 Pieces	Fresh Shiitake Mushrooms
	Flour	1–2 Ounces	Salad Oil
3 Slices	Eggplant		

Sauce for Glazing

1 Cup	Water	¼ Cup	Mirin (Sweet Rice Wine)
½ Cup	Shoyu	¼ Cup	Sugar
¼ Cup	Sake (Rice Wine)		

Combine above ingredients for sauce and bring to a boil for five minutes. Set aside. Makes approximately 2 cups.

Flour each piece of duck. Sauté duck in hot salad oil until both sides become golden brown. Rinse duck with tap water. Place duck in the same frying pan and add eggplant and shiitake mushrooms. Add approximately ½ cup of sauce. Simmer until sauce becomes thick, about five minutes. Place duck and vegetables neatly on platter and serve.

Agedashi Tofu (Deep Fried Tofu)

1 Piece	Small Block of Tofu, (3" X 3" X 2")	2–3 Cups	Salad Oil (for deep frying)

Garnish

½ Teaspoon	Grated Ginger	1 Teaspoon	Chopped Green Onion
1 Tablespoon	Grated Turnip		

Sauce

4 Ounces	Dashi Stock (Bonito Flake Stock)	1 Ounce	Mirin
		1 Ounce	Soy Sauce

Use an ounce ladle for measurements. Mix ingredients together.

Pat and dry tofu block. Deep fry until tofu surface becomes crispy, approximately 2–3 minutes. Drain oil. Place tofu in appropriate container and garnish with grated turnip, ginger and chopped onions. Pour sauce over tofu and serve. Sauce should be warm. Serve as an appetizer.

3660 ON THE RISE

(808) 737–1177 • 3660 Waialae Ave., Honolulu, Oahu 96816

A shared dream and the courage to take the risks to make the dream come true, were two things that Gale Ogawa and Russell Siu had in common. In a surprisingly short amount of time, they have created an extremely successful restaurant! Opened in September, 1992, 3660 on the Rise was voted "Best New Restaurant for 1993", by the readers of Honolulu Magazine. Then in 1994, 3660 won "Restaurant of the Year" and "Best Innovative Island Cuisine"!

Russell is the chef and creates an ever changing menu of innovative Euro–Island Cuisine. A popular appetizer is Ahi Katsu–Ahi wrapped in Nori and deep fried. Entree examples include: Salmon wrapped in angel hair potatoes; Chinese steamed fillet of Opakapaka, and New York Alaea topped with crisp onions.

They are known for large portions and great desserts. Russell's wife, Lisa, is the pastry chef who creates their irresistible sweet selections: Harlequin Creme Brulee–Vanilla Bean Custard and Chocolate Mousse glazed with a sugar crust, or Warm Chocolate Soufflé Cake. Luscious!

Both Gale and Russell grew up in Hawaii. Their approach to 3660's cuisine, Gale says, is "taking local food and adding a nice flair to it". They wanted to create an "upscale neighborhood restaurant," yet still have people feel comfortable just dropping by. But due to their tremendous success, I would recommend reservations.

Lunch Tuesday–Friday. $9.00–$13.00. Dinner Tuesday–Sunday. Entrees $17.00–$22.00.

Sake Seared Scallops

16	Sea Scallops (size:20–30 count per pound)	12 Ounces	Mesclun Mix of Greens
½ Cup	Sake	½ Package	Long Rice (Cellophane Noodles)
	Salt and Pepper	1 Tablespoon	Black Sesame Seeds
2 Ounces	Peanut Oil	1	Carrot

In a hot skillet add peanut oil to coat pan. Add scallops to pan. Season with salt and pepper. When the scallops are brown on one side, turn. (Make sure flame is on high). Let scallops fry for about a minute and then add sake. Let sake cook down until a dark glaze develops. Shake pan to coat scallops. Reserve on side.

Fry ¼ of the package of long rice and reserve on side. Boil the balance of the package of long rice. Cool immediately with cold water when done. When cool, drain thoroughly. Turn carrots through machine to make carrot noodles. Another alternative garnish would be to finely grate the carrots or cut into match stick size. Toss mesclun of greens with the peanut chili vinaigrette (recipe below). Do not drench greens.

Toss boiled noodles also with dressing. On a plate drizzle some dressing, add tossed noodles then mesclun of greens. Place 4 scallops on the plate surrounding the mesclun. Top with carrot noodles and dried noodles. Sprinkle with black sesame seeds and serve.

Peanut Chili Vinaigrette

2 Tabespoons	Peanut Butter	1 Tablespoon	Cilantro
½ Cup	Rice Vinegar	½ Teaspoon	Chili Paste
1 Tablespoon	Green Onion	1"	Lemon Grass
1 Teaspoon	Garlic	1 Cup	Salad Oil
¼ Cup	Chili Sauce		

Mix together in food processor.

For Lacquered Salmon with Lime Black Bean Sauce from 3660 on the Rise, see page 185.

The historic Waioli Tea Room is located in the beautiful and lush Manoa Valley, just a few minutes from the bustle of Honolulu. The Tea Room was built in 1921 and "served as a vocational training facility for young women in the Salvation Army Girls' Home". The Waioli Tea Room was known for their afternoon tea service and delicious baked goods. They provided meals for the military during World War II. And, in the 1950s through the 1970s, they were a popular place to dine.

After being refurbished, they reopened in 1993 to share a part of history with those of us fortunate enough to find them. The Tea Room continues to generate support for Salvation Army services. The garden setting is lovely and displays many palms, bird of paradise, heliconia, ti plants, ginger, and more. The chapel on the premises averages 17 weddings a day! I saw a bride and groom being photographed when I was there.

The Waioli Tea Room menu includes favorites such as Thai Chicken Curry, Eggplant Parmesan, and Mahimahi Dore. They feature fresh baked pies for dessert (coconut, macadamia nut, and banana cream). On Thursdays a Hawaiian lunch is featured with live Hawaiian music. Lunch Tuesday through Friday under $10.00. Lunch buffet Saturday and Sunday usually $12.00–$16.00. Dinner served Friday night only, features an Italian buffet for $13.95. Reservations preferred.

Vegetarian Pot Stickers

½ Cup	Cooked Basmati or other brown rice		2 Tablespoons	Black Olives, finely chopped
½ Cup	Tofu, mashed		1 Teaspoon	Fine Red Chili Pepper
2 Tablespoons	Fresh Basil, finely chopped			Sesame Oil to taste
3 Tablespoons	Shiitake Mushrooms, finely chopped			Oil for frying
2 Tablespoons	Tamari			Potsticker Wrappers, (round)

Combine Basmati rice, tofu, basil, mushrooms, black olives, tamari, pepper and sesame oil in a mixing bowl. Chill for at least 30 minutes. Fill potsticker wrappers and seal with water. Heat oil for frying in a non–stick pan with cover. Place filled potstickers in a pan and lightly brown, approximately 3 minutes. Add ½ cup of water to pan, cover and let steam until all water has evaporated. Serve with dipping sauce (recipe below).

Dipping Sauce

½ Cup	Grated Daikon Radish		3 Tablespoons	Lemon Juice
1 Cup	Diced Tomato		2 Tablespoons	Tamari
½ Teaspoon	Cumin Seed		2 Tablespoons	Fresh or Shiso Leaves, finely chopped
½ Teaspoon	Chili Powder			
2 Tablespoons	Chopped Green Onion			

Combine all ingredients in a glass bowl and set aside in the refrigerator over night.

Mango Pie

1	Unbaked 9" Pie Crust

Filling

2½ Cups	Thinly Sliced Mango (Peaches may also be used)		¼ Cup	Honey
			2 Tablespoons	Whole Wheat Flour
½ Cup	Unsweetened Coconut		½ Teaspoon	Cinnamon
			⅛ Teaspoon	Nutmeg

Gently combine and place into pie crust.

2	Eggs, or Egg Substitute		3/4 Cup	Honey
12 Ounces	Very Fresh Tofu		½ Teaspoon	Cinnamon
4 Ounces	Cream Cheese, or "Soya Kaas" substitute		¼ Teaspoon	Salt
			1½ Teaspoons	Vanilla

Mix in a blender until smooth. Gently pour blended ingredients over mango (or peach) combination. Do not stir. Bake at 350 degrees for 50–60 minutes.

Julie Yarbrough has created a unique theme for her restaurant, something unusual for Hawaii, a country garden concept—light, bright and cheerful. Julie has been an interior designer and has executed this fresh, springtime theme very well—the ceiling is even painted blue to look like sky. It's fun and charming. Julie's son, Tertius, manages the restaurant, and her daughter, Shay (who lives in San Francisco) did the graphics for Tulips.

Andrew Mc Coy is the executive chef. Julie explains that "He is responsible for incredible, innovative and creative nightly specials." Andrew started cooking at a very early age and is primarily self taught. He says, "I like to make food that people enjoy eating, from simple to elegant." Here are two examples of his delicious nightly specials: Fresh Onaga grilled and served with a mango lemon grass sauce and banana walnut chutney, or Veal Chop—char broiled then roasted in the oven with wild mushroom demi glacé and Maui Onion rings. Tulips signature item is Grilled Sea Scallops with sweet Thai chili–basil sauce and jasmine rice. For dessert try one of five daily specials. They include apple or peach crisp and chocolate bread pudding with espresso gelato, and raspberry sauce. Yum.

Dinner only, Tuesday through Sunday night. $13.00–$26.00. Call for reservations.

Pan–Seared Opakapaka Fillets with Macadamia Nut–Pesto and a Lobster Fried Rice

4	4 Ounce Fillets of Fresh Opakapaka

Pesto

5	Garlic Cloves	1 Cup	Fresh Basil
2 Ounces	Macadamia Nuts	½ Cup	Olive Oil
¼ Cup	Parmesan Cheese		Salt and Pepper

Mix together in food processor.

Lobster Fried Rice

8 Ounces	Rock Lobster Meat or substitute any other type of Shellfish	¼ Cup	Oyster Sauce
		4 Cups	Jasmine Rice, cooked (begin with 2 cups uncooked)
½ Each	Red and Yellow Bell Pepper, diced		
		4 Tablespoons	Soy Sauce
1	Green Onion, chopped	1 Tablespoon	Sesame Seed Oil
1	Maui Onion, diced	1 Tablespoon	Fresh Grated Ginger
½ Cup	Diced Mushrooms	1 Tablespoon	Fresh Chopped Garlic

Heat two pans, one with tablespoon olive oil, the other with sesame oil. Season fish fillets with Kosher salt and fresh ground pepper. Place in pan coated with olive oil. Cook until golden brown, turn and put into hot oven. Put garlic, ginger and lobster into pan coated with sesame oil, and sauté. Add remainder of vegetables and continue to stir until vegetables become cooked. Deglaze with sweet sake (mirin) and add cooked jasmine rice, oyster and soy sauce. Continue cooking until all ingredients are thoroughly mixed. Remove filets from oven and coat with pesto. Place under broiler for 1–3 minutes. Serve on lobster fried rice with garnish and vegetables of choice. Serves four.

For Double Chocolate Bread Pudding with Toasted Macadamia Nuts, Kahlua Creme Anglaise and Kona Coffee Gelato from Tulips, see page 186.

Kahala Moon is a wonderful upscale neighborhood restaurant. I enjoyed the feeling of the warm, comfortable, and inviting atmosphere, the blend of local and other clientele, and, of course, the excellent food.

Owner, Kelvin Ro grew up on Oahu. He knew in third grade what he wanted to do with his life. Kahala Moon is a representation of his mission, his dream. It's a creative expression of his desire to please and provide for others. It certainly pleased me. The beautiful art lining the walls changes monthly, featuring a new artist. The lovely flower arrangements that accent the room are created by Kelvin. And the beautiful Koa bar is also something to admire. Kahala Moon is the third restaurant Kelvin has opened in Hawaii; his experience and attention to detail and quality shows. Kahala Moon was awarded "Best New Restaurant" by Travel and Holiday Magazine. They were given four stars by Honolulu Magazine and voted "Best New Restaurant for 1995" by readers of the magazine.

Kelvin explains that the menu changes with the seasons, and is designed to bring out the natural flavors of the fine, fresh ingredients that are available in Hawaii. A lunch specialty is the Grilled Chicken Breast sandwich on housemade focaccia (Italian herb bread) with tropical fruit mustard. For dinner, specialties are: Pan Seared Scallops on Nalo greens with orange segments and crispy Maui onion rings, or Grilled Lamb Chops with caramelized onion potatoes and lemon–cilantro butter. And, they serve scrumptious desserts!

Live music is featured on Friday and Saturday nights. Lunch Monday–Friday. $8.00–$11.00. Dinner nightly. Entrees $16.00–$25.00. Call for reservations.

Asparagus Ginger Risotto

10 Ounces	Aborio Rice (type of rice used for making Risotto)	4 Cups	Chicken Broth
1	Thyme Sprig	10	Large Spinach Leaves
1	Bay Leaf	10	Asparagus Spears
5 Ounces	White Onion	2 Ounces	Butter
1 Teaspoon	Fresh Ginger	2 Ounces	Grated Parmesan Cheese

Fine dice the onion and rough chop the spinach. Par boil, cool and chop the asparagus spears into 1 inch pieces and fine mince the ginger. Then, in a shallow thick bottom pot, slowly sauté the onion, bay leaf, thyme and ginger in 1 ounce of whole butter for 3 minutes. Add the rice and coat well with the sautéed mixture. When the outside of the grain becomes clear, add 1½ cups chicken broth. Add more broth as the rice absorbs the liquid while stirring constantly. Test the rice by rolling the grain on the roof of your mouth by using your tongue. When the grain dissolves completely, it is finished and should have a light, soupy consistency. Fold in the spinach and par cooked asparagus. Finish with the rest of the butter and parmesan cheese. Adjust the seasoning with salt and white pepper. Serve on the side for a starch or by itself as a main course. Serves five (6 ounce portions).

Sake Steamed Clams with Miso, Ginger, Tomato and Linguini

7	New Zealand Clams (Cockles), scrubbed	¼ Teaspoon	Garlic, minced
5 Ounces	Linguini	2 Tablespoons	Butter
2 Ounces	Sake	1 Tablespoon	Orange Juice
2 Ounces	Fish Stock	1 Tablespoon	Sun–Dried Tomatoes, chopped
1 Teaspoon	Miso	1 Tablespoon	Green Onion, chopped
¼ Teaspoon	Ginger, minced	1 Pinch	Black Pepper, ground

Pre-cook the linguini to al dente, drain and toss with a little oil so as not to stick. In a heavy bottomed pot combine all ingredients except the linguini and green onion, cover and place on high heat. Cook for an additional 30 seconds after clams open and remove from heat. Remove clams and arrange in pasta bowl. Add linguini and green onion to broth and place over fire until heated through. Mound pasta in center of bowl and spoon sauce over and around. Garnish with green onion. Serves one.

Lisbeth Holmefjord moved to Oahu in 1987 after living in Italy for three years. She met Shari Sarabi. He co−owned an Italian restaurant on Oahu. Lisbeth explained that in her case, "the way to a woman's heart is through her stomach." Lisbeth and Shari got married, and now have three children and two successful restaurants–Spiedini and Baci Due.

Shari is the executive chef and creative force for both restaurants. He uses fresh organic produce whenever possible, and veal from Switzerland which has no hormones and is treated in a more humane way. Raviolis, gnocchi, and all the pastas are handmade. Lisbeth says, "Not one single dish is precooked," and therefore they can accommodate special requests.

Spiedini is located at the Koko Marina on Kaapa Pond (an ancient fish pond for Hawaiian Kings). Boat docks are reserved for guests and outdoor seating by the water is available.

Their delicious signature appetizer is Grilled Shrimp with lime, mint, and feta cheese. The signature entrée is Fettuccini with grilled fish, mussels, calamari and vegetables tossed with extra virgin olive oil, parmesan and romano cheeses.

On weekends live Italian music is featured.

Dinner nightly. Entrees $11.00–$30.00. Sunday brunch. Call for reservations.

Baci Due, located at 3196 Waialae Ave., Honolulu, (808) 735−5899, is small and intimate. Lunch Monday through Friday. Dinner Monday through Saturday. Call for reservations.

Bruschetta

3 Cups	Chopped Ripe Tomato		¼ Cup	Loose Chopped Parsley
½ Small	Onion, chopped		¼ Cup	Extra Virgin Olive Oil
5 Cloves	Chopped Garlic			Salt and Pepper to Taste
½ Cup	Loose Chopped Basil			

Slice day–old baguette (firm bread) into 12 pieces. Mix all the ingredients in a big bowl (except the bread). Toast the bread, preferably on a charcoal broiler or barbecue. Spoon the mix onto the bread, and serve immediately. Serves six.

Bucatini All Matricana

12 Ounces	Fresh Tomato Sauce		8–10 Ounces	Pasta Bucatini
¼	Onion, chopped		2 Ounces	Parmesan Cheese
2	Cloves Chopped Garlic			Hot Crushed Pepper to Taste
1½ Ounces	Olive Oil			Salt and Pepper to Taste
3 Ounces	Pacetta (Italian Bacon)			

Bring a large pot of water to boil. Add olive oil. Add chopped onion, garlic, chopped panchetta, salt and pepper and hot pepper in a saucepan. Sauté for 3 to 4 minutes. Add tomato sauce and simmer for 3 to 5 minutes. Put pasta in water for 2 minutes and strain all water. Add sauce and cheese to pasta. Serves two.

ASSAGGIO

(808) 261–2772 • 354 Uluniu Street, Kailua, Oahu 96734
(808) 623–5115 • 95–1249 Meheula Parkway, Mililani, Oahu 96789

Assaggio in Kailua was highly recommended to me before I even arrived on Oahu. When I did arrive in the Kailua area, I found out that it is indeed a popular place to enjoy a fine Italian meal featuring fine quality ingredients from Italy combined with fresh herbs (grown in a garden just outside the restaurant) to create authentic dishes served with fresh baked Italian bread.

Assaggio means "to taste". There are now 3 locations on Oahu where you can experience a taste of owner/chef Thomas Ky's fine Italian cuisine. (One of the restaurants is named Paesano—see address below.) Many friends and family members work at the restaurants. Thomas' wife, Siri, expressed how much Thomas loves to cook and explained that they put a lot of heart into their work.

Each location offers deli items available for take out daily, including their Italian bread, their own Marinara sauce, homemade Italian meatballs and sausage (sold by the pound), and a variety of pastas.

Assaggio and Paesano offer a wide variety of tempting items on their menu and feature daily specials, such as Steak Capri—calamari steak topped with 4 jumbo shrimp, melted mozzarella cheese, with a white wine, butter, and mushroom sauce, served with linguini. Homemade Hot Antipasto is a favorite appetizer (recipe at right). Each entrée is offered in small or regular size portions. Homemade Tiramisu is recommended for dessert and an extensive wine list features wines from Italy, Chile, Germany, France and California.

Kailua location serves lunch Monday through Friday. Dinner nightly. Entrees $8.00–$18.00.
Mililani location serves lunch and dinner daily.
Paesano is located at the Manoa Marketplace, Honolulu, Oahu 96822 (808) 988–5923.

Hot Antipasto (Appetizer)

3 Pieces	Mussels on the Half Shell	¼ Teaspoon	Kosher Salt
3 Pieces	Fresh Clams	¼ Teaspoon	Black Pepper
4 Pieces	Jumbo Shrimp (size: 13/15 per pound)	½ Teaspoon	Rouxe (thickening agent); ratio 1:1 of Butter:Flour
6 Pieces	Julienne Calamari	2 Ounces	White Wine
1 Teaspoon	Minced Garlic	2 Ounces	Butter, softened
2 Teaspoons	Paprika		Olive Oil
1 Teaspoon	Cayenne Pepper		

Heat pan, add olive oil, garlic, mussels, clams, shrimp, calamari, paprika, cayenne pepper, salt, pepper and sauté. When three quarters cooked, add rouxe and white wine. Reduce for 15 seconds and add butter. Place in a casserole dish or arrange on plate. Serves one.

Chicken Assaggio

5 Ounces	Julienne Chicken	6	Slices Pepperoncini
1 Tablespoon	Minced Garlic	8	Black Olive Halves
½ Teaspoon	Kosher Salt	4	Slices Mushrooms
¼ Teaspoon	Black Pepper	2 Ounces	White Wine
1 Tablespoon	Fresh Basil	1½ Ounces	Chicken Stock
4 Pieces	Roasted Bell Pepper, sliced (¼ Pepper)	2 Ounces	Butter, softened

Heat pan. When hot add olive oil, julienne chicken, minced garlic, kosher salt, black pepper. Sauté. When chicken is three quarters done, add roasted bell pepper, sliced pepperoncini, black olives, sliced mushrooms, and basil. Finish cooking until chicken is done. Add white wine, reduce for about 30 seconds. Add chicken stock and softened butter. Pour over your favorite pasta. Serves one.

CINNAMON'S RESTAURANT
(808) 261-8724 • 315 Uluniu Street, Kailua, Oahu 96734

When I asked where there was a good place to have breakfast in Kailua, I was told Cinnamon's. What I discovered was a very homey, quaint and comfortable place with a friendly staff that shared lots of smiles. Cinnamon's features a wide variety of choices in a smoke free environment. It is owned and operated by Norman "Puna" Nam and Bonnie "Cricket" Nam, who explained that they serve "real food, made from scratch, non-processed, with low fat and fat free choices." And their talented chef Carsic Green who opened the restaurant with them in 1985 is now a partner of their wonderful restaurant.

Specialties for breakfast include: delicious Eggs Benedict, offered traditional, vegie, or with Mahi Mahi. Sausages, and unique pancakes (carrot, gingerbread, lemon...) are also available. Lunch features their award winning Portuguese Bean Soup, or try the popular Chicken Cashew Sandwich. A favorite for dinner is the Chicken Curry which is served with seven condiments, including freshly grated coconut, or their Roasted Turkey and Dressing, or Scampi. Desserts are fresh baked and are always changing—French Apple pie, Chocolate Mocha Cake, mmm.

The theme of Cinnamon's is based on a wonderful fairy tale about a helpful little bear named Cinnamon.

Breakfast 7:00 a.m. through 2:00 p.m. daily. $3.00–$9.00. Lunch daily. $4.00–$8.00. Sunday brunch. Dinner Thursday, Friday and Saturday. $8.00–$17.00. Reservations recommended for six or more. Turn into parking lot across from Pizza Hut. Cinnamon's is located in the back left corner.

Pumpkin Pancakes

½ Cup	Canned Solid Pack Pumpkin		⅛ Teaspoon	Nutmeg
¼ Teaspoon	Cinnamon		1 Tablespoon	Granulated Sugar
⅛ Teaspoon	Ginger		1⅓ Cups	Water
Dash	Cloves		2½ Cups	Pancake Mix

Mix first 7 ingredients. Add your dry mix (don't over mix). Get grill ready at 375 degrees. Spray grill with a non–stick spray. Drop 5" circles on the grill and turn after bubbles cover the top. Enjoy pancakes topped with powdered sugar. Yummy!

Cinnamon's Bread Pudding

Start with 4 sliced cinnamon rolls or other sweet bread to loosely fill a buttered 8" X 8" square baking dish. Mix the following ingredients together and pour over bread slices.

4 Cups	Milk		¾ Cup	Sugar
4	Beaten Eggs		½ Teaspoon	Cinnamon
½ Teaspoon	Salt		1 Teaspoon	Vanilla

Put the smaller pan into a 9" X 13" pan. Add 1" of water. Bake at 350 degrees for 1½ hours or until golden brown. Serve warm with rum raisin sauce (recipe below).

Rum Raisin Sauce

1 Cup	Sugar		¼ Cup	Rum
2 Tablespoons	Cornstarch		¼ Cup	Butter or Margarine
¼ Teaspoon	Salt		2 Teaspoons	Vanilla
1¾ Cups	Boiling Water		¾ Cup	Raisins

Combine sugar and cornstarch in a saucepan. Mix in salt and gradually add boiling water stirring constantly. Add rum and raisins and continue to stir bringing mixture to a boil. Simmer 5 minutes. Remove from heat and blend in butter and vanilla. Serve warm.

The first Chart House was opened on the Fourth of July in 1961 in Aspen, Colorado by surf legends Joey Cabell and Buzzy Bent (they also loved to ski).

The Haiku Gardens Chart House was recommended as being one of the nicest places to eat in the Kaneohe–Kailua area. The grounds are absolutely beautiful, lush and tropical, serene and romantic, with a view of the Koolau Mountains. The fabulous garden that the restaurant overlooks features a large lily pond and

The view from the Chart House

a gazebo. Many weddings and ceremonies take place there. I saw a traditional Hawaiian wedding, with ceremonial chants and dancing, in progress when I was there.

The dining area has a casual, open air atmosphere, with the servers wearing Hawaiian print shirts and dresses. A great salad bar, and warm sourdough and squaw breads are served with dinner. Signature items include Herb–steamed artichokes, Teriyaki sirloin steak, Grilled Ahi, and their decadent and popular Mud Pie for dessert.

The Haleiwa Chart House is also recommended, with views of Haleiwa Harbor. Lunch and dinner are served. Located at 66–011 Kamehameha Highway, Haleiwa, (808) 637–8005.

Haiku Gardens Chart House serves dinner only, nightly. $15.00–$25.00.

Chart House Mud Pie

4½ Ounces	Chocolate Wafers
¼ Cup	Butter, melted
1 Gallon	Coffee Ice Cream, soft
1½ Cups	Fudge Sauce
	Diced Almonds

Crush wafers and add butter, mix well. Press into a 9" pie plate. Cover with soft coffee ice cream. Top with cold fudge sauce. (It helps to put the fudge sauce in the freezer for a while to make spreading easier.) Store the Mud Pie in the freezer for approximately 10 hours before serving. Slice into eight portions and serve on chilled dessert plates. Top with whipped cream and diced almonds.

Chart House Bleu Cheese Dressing

¾ Cup	Sour Cream
½ Teaspoon	Dry Mustard
½ Teaspoon	Black Pepper
½ Teaspoon	Salt
⅓ Teaspoon	Garlic Powder
1 Teaspoon	Worcestershire Sauce
1⅓ Cups	Mayonnaise
4 Ounces	Bleu Cheese (imported Danish, crumbled)

Combine the first six ingredients and blend for two minutes at low speed. Add mayonnaise and blend for 30 seconds at low speed, then increase speed to medium and blend an additional two minutes. Slowly add the bleu cheese and blend at low speed no longer than four minutes. Refrigerate for 24 hours before serving. Yields 2 ½ cups.

CROUCHING LION INN

(808) 237-8511 • 51-666 Kamehameha, Kaaawa, Oahu 96730

The drive to the Crouching Lion Inn (heading north along the east side of Oahu) is beautiful. Lush greenery surrounds you and mountains jut almost straight up from the ground. The Inn was originally built as a family residence in 1926, and was converted to a restaurant in 1957. If you look at the hillside behind the restaurant, you can see a landmark rock formation in the form of a crouching lion. The Legend of the Crouching Lion can be heard at the restaurant where they sometimes have a story teller sharing legends and spirit tales of Old Hawaii. I enjoyed my visit there and felt the aloha and authentic Hawaiian hospitality. The manager, Frances "Fattie" Bryant (who has worked there for 20 years!) sat and talked with me as I ate. Outdoor dining is very pleasant, with a great view of Kahana Bay.

The Crouching Lion Inn offers salads, hamburgers, sandwiches, and entrées (Mahi Mahi, Kalua Pork, and fresh Island fish purchased daily at local fish auctions, Shrimp Salad...) and their own homemade buns. For dinner, they are known for their Slavonic Steak. Other choices include Seafood, Pacific Rim, and vegetarian selections. Desserts are prepared daily in their bakery. Polynesian drinks are popular here too, including a "Spider Lily" and "The Lion's Roar".

I was impressed by the great selection of art by well known artists of Hawaii featured in the gallery downstairs.

Open daily. Lunch $6.75–$11.00. Dinner $15.00–$24.00.

Honey Garlic Shrimp

1⅓ Pounds	Large Cleaned Shrimp

Batter

2 Cups	Flour	2	Eggs
⅓ Cup	Baking Powder	1⅓ Cups	Water

Mix ingredients together to make batter.

Dip shrimp in batter, deep fry until golden brown. Top with the honey–garlic sauce. Serve as an appetizer or side dish.

Honey-Garlic Sauce

1⅔ Pounds	Honey	2 Teaspoons	Sesame Seeds
2 Tablespoons +		2 Teaspoons	Chopped Garlic
2 Teaspoons	Sherry		

Combine all ingredients.

Slavonic Steak for Two

2	14 Ounce Tenderloin Steaks	Italian Seasonings
	Salad Oil	Fresh Coursely Ground Pepper

Marinate the steaks in a mixture of salad oil, Italian seasonings and pepper for 2 hours or to your liking. Charbroil marinated steaks. Serve thinly sliced on a sizzling platter of garlic butter.

Whether you are in Haleiwa on the North Shore of Oahu, or in the Kailua–Kona area of the Big Island of Hawaii, Jameson's is recommended as a great place to relax, have a refreshing drink and enjoy good food. Both locations have spectacular sunset views over the ocean.

Owner, Ed Greene, opened the first Jameson's in 1975. They feature daily specials with, of course, lots of fresh seafood. The specialty of the house is Opakapaka poached in white wine, topped with a garlic hollandaise sauce. Baked Stuffed Shrimp is very popular for a dinner choice also. The Jameson's hamburger is a hot item for lunch. They make their own chiffon pies for dessert, with intriguing flavors such as Kona Coffee, Chocolate Mousse, and Grasshopper.

Debbie Ahern, Ed's wife, has a beautiful gift shop called Outrigger Trading Company at the Haleiwa location. It features a quality selection of crafts by local artists. Be sure to pick up some delicious and creamy fudge from The Fudge Works there. Connected to the gift store is Galerie Lassen, featuring an impressive collection of fine art by Christian Reese Lassen and other island artists.

When the waves get big on the North Shore of Oahu, Jameson's offers a fabulous view of the excitement! Ed told me that people call from all around the island to check the surf and weather report.

The Haleiwa location has an open air pub that serves lunch all afternoon. Upstairs is an air conditioned dining room for casual fine dining, five nights a week.

Call for dinner reservations and information. Pub, lunch daily, and dinner two nights a week. $6.00–$13.00. Weekend brunch. Upstairs dining, dinner only, five nights a week. $13.00–$25.00.

The Kona restaurant is located at 77–6452 Alii Drive, Kailua-Kona, Hawaii 96740, (808) 329–3195. Lunch Monday through Friday. Dinner nightly.

Baked Stuffed Shrimp

48   Large Shrimp, butterflied

Stack two shrimp on top of each other. Place wedges of stuffing on top of shrimp and place on baking pan. Bake for 5 minutes or until shrimp are cooked. Top with Hollandaise sauce (recipe below).

Cheese Sauce

12 Ounces	Milk		Dash	Dry Mustard
2 Ounces	Butter		Dash	White Pepper
2 Ounces	Flour		Dash	Worcestershire Sauce
Dash	Salt		14 Ounces	Sharp Cheddar Cheese

Heat milk, salt, pepper, and Worcestershire sauce in a large pot. Mix flour and mustard together, then add butter. Mix well. When milk mixture comes to a boil, add flour mixture. Mix in well. Turn stove off. Add shredded cheese. Mix well.

Stuffing

2 Ounces	Onion, minced		¼ Pound	Dungeness Crab Meat
1 Ounce	Celery, minced		¼ Pound	White Fish (steamed)
¼ Ounce	Parsley, minced		½ Pound	Bread Crumbs
¼ Cup	Butter		1 Pint	Cheese Sauce (recipe
¼ Ounce	Sherry			above.)

Sauté together, onions and celery in butter until tender. Then add parsley and sherry; mix well. In a large mixing bowl, combine all other ingredients. Mix together well. Portion and form mix into 24 wedges.

Hollandaise Sauce

24 Ounces	Drawn Butter		⅛ Teaspoon	Cayenne Pepper
5	Egg Yolks		1 Tablespoon	Lemon Juice

In a double boiler, heat egg yolks while stirring. Remove from heat and then slowly add butter while mixing. Add pepper and lemon juice. Mix in well.

For Salmon Paté from Jameson's, see page 185.

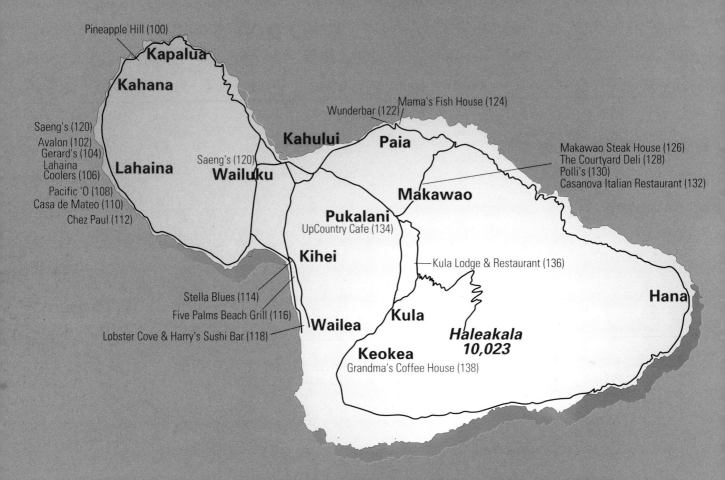

Pineapple Hill (100)

Kapalua

Kahana

Mama's Fish House (124)

Wunderbar (122)

Saeng's (120)

Avalon (102)
Gerard's (104)
Lahaina
Coolers (106)

Pacific 'O (108)
Casa de Mateo (110)

Chez Paul (112)

Kahului

Paia

Lahaina

Saeng's (120)

Wailuku

Makawao Steak House (126)
The Courtyard Deli (128)
Polli's (130)
Casanova Italian Restaurant (132)

Makawao

Pukalani
UpCountry Cafe (134)

Kihei

Kula Lodge & Restaurant (136)

Stella Blues (114)

Five Palms Beach Grill (116)

Wailea

Kula

Hana

Lobster Cove & Harry's Sushi Bar (118)

Keokea
Grandma's Coffee House (138)

**Haleakala
10,023**

Maui

The Valley Isle

Cuisines Featured

Expansive views of Lanai, Molokai, and captivating sunsets over the ocean are seen from Pineapple Hill. "Maka'oi'oi" (sharp eyes) is the name of this charming, historic plantation home that Pineapple Hill Restaurant has resided in since 1964. The home was owned by the late D. T. Fleming, who was one of the early pioneers in establishing pineapples, mangoes, lychee and other exotic plants and trees on Maui. "He who plants a tree, plants love," he stated. Lots of love was planted here—a mile long lane of majestic Norfolk Pines (that he planted over 80 years ago) lead to the restaurant, where you can now enjoy casual dining in a pleasant and historic atmosphere.

The specialty of the house is Shrimp Tahitian—large prawns seasoned and baked in the shell with wine, herbs and cheese. Other popular choices include chicken "Pineapple Hill" Polynesian—roasted with a guava glaze, served in a pineapple boat, and Papeete Steamed Fish which won second prize for seafood at the 1994 "Taste of Lahaina". Dinners are served with soup or salad, fresh vegetables and rolls. Desserts include Baked Papaya Tahitian (a first prize winner at the 1994 "Taste of Lahaina") and home-made Maui Lime Pie, both baked with Tahitian Vanilla Beans for great flavor!

Dinner nightly. $12.00–$30.00. Call for reservations. From Lahaina go north on Highway 30, turn left at the Kapalua sign onto Office Road, drive 400 feet, turn left. They offer courtesy parking for your convenience.

Chicken Polynesian

6	Fryer Range Chicken Breasts, 10 ounces each		2 Tablespoons	Minced Ginger
2	Medium Pineapples		1 Sprig	Fresh Thyme
6 Ounces	Coconut Milk		¼ Teaspoon	White Pepper
6 Ounces	Guava Puree		2 Ounces	Grenadine
6 Ounces	Pineapple Juice		2 Ounces	Tawny Port
2 Cups	Chicken Broth		8 Ounces	Mandarin Oranges
2 Tablespoons	Minced Garlic		1 Ounce	Coconut Flakes

For sauce: Combine coconut milk, guava puree, pineapple juice, chicken broth, ginger, garlic, thyme, pepper, grenadine and port in a sauce pan and reduce to one cup. For pineapple boats: Cut pineapples lengthwise into six pieces with crowns attached. Remove meat to create six "boats". Save two cups of meat for garnishing. To prepare chicken: Preheat oven to 350 degrees. Rinse chicken, drain and pat dry. Season with salt and pepper. Place in a roasting pan and into the oven for 20–30 minutes until skin is browned and chicken is done. Assemble by placing each breast into each "boat" and cover with 2–3 ounces of sauce. Garnish with pineapple chunks, mandarin oranges and coconut flakes. A good accompaniment for this dish is a shichimi rice pilaf along with a stir fry of sugar snap peas, carrots and Maui onions. Serves six.

Chicken Long Rice Soup

1	Fryer, 2 Pounds		1	Medium Maui Onion, julienned
1 Quart	Chicken Broth			
1 Quart	Water		2 Packages	Long Rice, 1¾ ounces each, soak in water until soft, about one half hour
1	2 Inch Piece Ginger, peeled and crushed			
6 Cloves	Garlic, peeled and crushed			Salt and Pepper to Taste
8 Ounces	Oyster Mushrooms, julienned		3 Stalks	Scallions cut on bias for garnish

In a large stock pot, combine chicken broth, water, fryer (rinsed), ginger and garlic. Simmer 1 hour until tender. Reserve both chicken and stock. Strain stock to remove unwanted particles and skim fat off top. Remove skin from chicken and shred meat. To prepare long rice, cut long rice with a pair of clean kitchen shears. Drain water through colander. Sauté onions and mushrooms until tender. Add all ingredients, except scallions, and simmer 10–15 minutes. Serve in bowls, garnish with scallions. Serves eight.

AVALON RESTAURANT
(808) 667–5559 • 844 Front Street, Lahaina, Maui 96761

Avalon is a dream come true for Mark and Judy Ellman, who opened the restaurant in 1988. Mark, who is a self taught chef, has been featured in Food & Wine, House and Garden, and Bon Appetit, among other publications. He's even been on the "Today" show, where he cooked a Whole Fresh Opakapaka (which is on the Avalon menu). His creativity and innovative dishes are impressive.

Mark's love of diversity in flavors began when he and Judy had their own catering company, "Can't Rock & Roll, But Sure Can Cook". He needed to accommodate the tastes of many talented clients such as Earth Wind and Fire, the Beach Boys, Moody Blues, and more.

Mark's cuisine features many of the fresh ingredients available in Hawaii, and is influenced by California, Indonesia, Vietnam, Thailand, China, and Japan.

Avalon is highly recommended on the island. It has a pleasant courtyard setting, as well as intimate open air rooms for dining. A lot of great, colorful art decorates the walls.

Their signature dish is Chili Seared Salmon Tiki Style—a layered salad of mashed potatoes, eggplant, salmon, greens, mango and tomato salsa with a plum vinaigrette. The Asian Pasta, made with shrimp, clams, scallops and fresh island fish, is superb. Vegetarian selections are offered as well as steaks. And to finish off whichever fabulous entrée you choose, the Caramel Miranda is heavenly. I shared it with a friend—an excellent way to end a meal.

Lunch Monday through Saturday. $8.00–$14.00. Dinner daily. Entrees $10.00–$28.00. Call for reservations.

Duck Lumpia with a Kona Gold Orange Sauce

4 Ounces	Cooked Duck Meat, shredded	1 Tablespoon	Chopped Mint
1 Ounce	Bean Sprouts	1 Tablespoon	Chopped Cilantro
½ Ounce	Chopped Garlic	1 Tablespoon	Chives
½ Ounce	Chopped Ginger		Salt and Pepper
1 Ounce	Chopped Broiled Eggplant	2 Tablespoons	Macadamia Nuts
			Lumpia Wrappers

Combine all ingredients in a bowl and place in lumpia wrappers to make Spring Rolls. Fry for 3–5 minutes, drain and pat dry. Slice on the bias.

Kona Gold Orange Sauce

1 Cup	Orange Juice	1	Lime Leaf
1 Tablespoon	Chili Sauce	½ Cup	Water
1	Lemon Grass, sliced	3 Tablespoons	Cilantro, chopped

Combine all ingredients except cilantro in a sauce pan. Simmer to reduce by one–half. Add cilantro. Serve with lumpia.

Caramel Miranda

4 Ounces Macadamia Nut Ice Cream, homemade or Häagan-Daz

Any 4 to 6 of the Following:

2 Ounces	Fresh Coconut, toasted	2 Ounces	Blackberries
2 Ounces	Maui Pineapple Cubes	2 Ounces	Cherimoya
2 Ounces	Star Fruit	2 Ounces	Apple Banana
2 Ounces	Raspberries	2 Ounces	Durian
2 Ounces	Long Stem Strawberries	2 Ounces	Figs

(You may also use any other combination of fresh fruit that sounds appealing.)

Caramel Sauce

1½ Cups	Sugar	3 Ounces	Heavy Cream
⅔ Cup	Water	1 Teaspoon	Butter
1 Teaspoon	Cream of Tartar		

Whisk together in a heavy saucepan sugar, water, and cream of tartar, over high heat until coppery brown. Remove from heat and whisk in cream until cool. Whisk in butter. Keep at room temperature. Lace sauce on oven proof plate. Sprinkle fruit over caramel and heat until hot. Remove. Spoon ice cream in center. Serve immediately.

GERARD'S RESTAURANT

(808) 661–8939 • 174 Lahainaluna Rd., Lahaina, Maui 96761

Gerard Reversade, chef and owner of Gerard's, is truly an artist with food. He is always creating, even in his sleep. Growing up in France, he began his profession at 14. At an even earlier age he grew his own vegetable garden, cooked crepes, and baked pastries. Having come to Hawaii in 1973, he now graces Maui with his incredible talent.

Gerard has created what he calls a "pure and sincere French restaurant." It's very authentic. He combines French techniques with fresh local ingredients to create outstanding dishes. Bon Appétit called Gerard's "Maui's Little French Jewel." Gerard's was rated as one of Hawaii's top 10 restaurants in "Who's Who in America's Restaurants".

The atmosphere is very inviting and romantic. Whether you choose to dine on the classic porch or inside, the comfortable wicker chairs, linen tablecloths, and stained glass windows create a wonderful French Country Victorian charm.

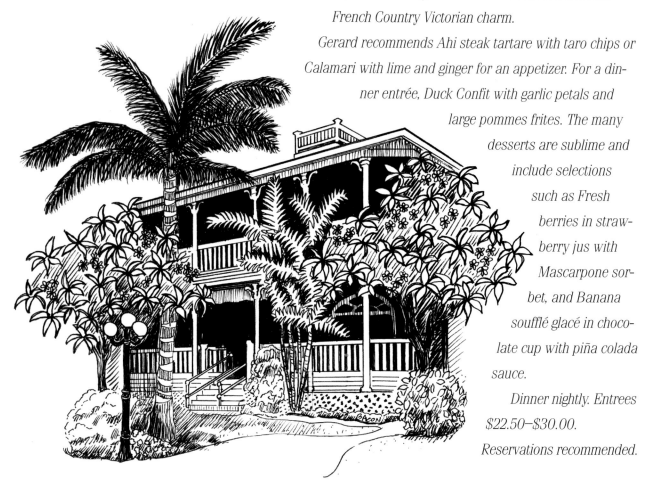

Gerard recommends Ahi steak tartare with taro chips or Calamari with lime and ginger for an appetizer. For a dinner entrée, Duck Confit with garlic petals and large pommes frites. The many desserts are sublime and include selections such as Fresh berries in strawberry jus with Mascarpone sorbet, and Banana soufflé glacé in chocolate cup with piña colada sauce.

Dinner nightly. Entrees $22.50–$30.00. Reservations recommended.

Calamari with Lime and Ginger

3 Pounds	Calamari, cleaned, gutted and sliced ¼" thick	1 Stalk	Scallion, sliced ¼" thick
1 Ounce	Fresh Ginger, peeled and finely diced		Salt and Freshly Ground Pepper
3	Limes, peeled and sectioned	3 Teaspoons	Sesame Oil
		6 Tablespoons	Peanut Oil

When ready to serve, heat 2 thick sauté pans and add the peanut oil. Season calamari. Sauté on high heat to retain tenderness and crispness. Cook only a few seconds. Turn off heat. Transfer to hot plates. Decorate with lime sections, ginger, scallions and pour sesame oil over. Serve with steamed rice as an appetizer or lunch. Serves six.

Tarte Tatin with Mango

Dough

8 Ounces	Flour	3 Ounces	Ice Water
5 Ounces	Butter	1 Ounce	Sugar
1	Egg	Pinch	Salt

Make dough by forming a well with the flour. Add all remaining dough ingredients. Mix well and let rest 1 hour.

8	Large Mangoes	Additional 1 Ounce Butter
1 Ounce	Raw Sugar	

Lightly caramelize the raw sugar and butter and pour into a pie plate. Peel and cut mango in large wedges, and put wedges on top of caramelized sugar/butter. Roll out dough ⅛" thick, large enough to cover the mango and the pie plate. Bake 30 minutes at 450 degrees. Serve warm, turned upside down. Can be served with a scoop of coconut ice cream and candied ginger. Serves eight.

For creative, fresh and exciting food, go to Lahaina Coolers, where their motto is: "Life's too short to eat boring food!" They offer a wide range of fun foods to choose from for every meal. Owners Gail Coe and Nickolai Mathison opened Lahaina Coolers in 1989. Each entrée is made fresh to order. They like to say, "Yes!" to special requests. Gail says, "If we have it, we'll be happy to do it." All dishes can be prepared vegetarian. Small sizes are also available, so you can try more adventures in taste.

Gail told me that their fresh fish for the evening is usually delivered around 4:00 p.m. by bike, just off the boat. And, hanging in their restaurant, along with the surf boards, is a replica of the largest Marlin (955 pounds!) caught at Lahaina. It's a state record, and was caught by a woman.

Lahaina Coolers is known for their unique pastas and pizzas. Their Evil Jungle Pasta is exquisite. I didn't want to stop eating it, the flavors were so good! Other favorites include: Fresh Fish Tacos, Coolers Thai salad with peanut–coconut–mint dressing, Moroccan Chicken Spinach Enchiladas and more! Breakfast favorites include: Breakfast Burrito with black beans and rice, four versions of Eggs Benedict, and a Mediterranean Omelet. Try a Chocolate Taco, filled with tropical fruit and berry "salsa" for dessert, or the Riviera Banana Split.

Open every day from 7:00 a.m. to 12:00 Midnight. Breakfast $3.00–$8.00. Lunch $5.50–$9.00. Dinner $5.50–$15.00.

Evil Jungle Pasta

Peanut Sauce

2 Cups	Peanuts	2 Ounces	Peanut Oil
2 Tablespoons	Soy Sauce	3 Tablespoons	White Vinegar
1½ Teaspoons	Thai Chili Oil	1 Teaspoon	White Pepper
1 Teaspoon	Salt	½ Cup	Coconut Syrup
½ Cup	Water		

Puree peanuts to a paste in food processor, then add other ingredients. Sauce should be pourable.

2 Ounces	Cooking Oil	12 Ounces	Sliced Chicken Breast
4 Ounces	White Wine	8 Ounces	Green & Red Pepper slices
8 Ounces	White Onion, sliced		Salt and Pepper to Taste
8 Ounces	Peanut Sauce	12 Ounces	Cream

Sauté chicken in oil. Splash with wine to deglaze. Add peppers and onion, then peanut sauce, cream, and season. When thoroughly hot, add:

Linguini, cooked al dente

Toss thoroughly. Garnish with:

Roasted Peanuts	**Carrot Slivers**
Green Onions	**Toasted Sesame Seeds**

Serves four.

For Spinach and Feta Cheese Quesadillas from Lahaina Coolers, see page 187.

Pacific'O is the perfect place to enjoy a relaxing lunch on the beach or a romantic sunset dinner looking out over the beautiful Pacific Ocean. It is small and intimate, with casual fine dining offered on the lanai under umbrellas, or in the open air restaurant. Their cuisine is fresh and creative. Co–owners/operators Stephan Bel–Robert (from France) and Louis Coulombe (from Quebec) met when working for other restaurants on Maui. When this great location became available, they decided to jump in and create their own restaurant. Chef James McDonald joined them bringing experience from the Ritz Carlton and Westin Hotels.

The food is a blending of French and Pacific Rim cuisines using local products–fruits, herbs, mushrooms and fresh Hawaiian fish. As Stephan says,

"There are no limits to Pacific Rim Cuisine...no rules, it's more fun than traditional French cooking."

Chef James McDonald created their award winning Shrimp Won Ton appetizer, prawns and basil won tons, served with a spicy sweet and sour sauce and Hawaiian salsa. Popular entrées include: Banana "Imu Style" Fish–fresh fish grilled in a banana leaf with lemon grass pesto and vanilla bean sauce, or the Sesame Crust Lamb–with roasted macadamia nut sauce and mango/pineapple chutney.

Live jazz is featured Thursday, Friday and Saturday nights...right on the beach ...under the stars...It's fabulous!

Open daily. Lunch $6.00–$12.00. Dinner entrées $15.00–$23.00. Call for reservations.

Shrimp Won Ton Served with a Spicy Sweet and Sour Sauce and a Hawaiian Salsa

Won Ton Marinade

1 Cup	Low Salt Soy Sauce	2 Stalks	Chopped Lemon Grass
1 Cup	Sesame Oil	2 Bulbs	Ginger Root
1 Cup	Loosely Packed Fresh Cilantro	1	Egg

Place all ingredients in a blender and process. Pour over peeled shrimp and let stand for 15 minutes.

Sweet and Sour Sauce

1 Cup	Sugar	1 Teaspoon	Red Chili Flakes
1 Cup	Red Wine Vinegar	1 Stick	Cinnamon
1 Tablespoon	Low Salt Soy Sauce	1 Teaspoon	Ground Cinnamon

Place all ingredients in a sauce pot and simmer for 20 minutes.

Hawaiian Salsa

2	Large Ripe Mangoes, peeled and diced (Papaya or Pineapple may be substituted)	1	Medium Onion, peeled and diced
		½ Cup	Loosely Packed Fresh Cilantro, coarsely chopped

Place all ingredients in a bowl and mix gently.

Won Ton

24	Won Ton Wrappers	24 Leaves	Fresh Sweet Basil
6 Ounces	Hoisin Sauce, in a squirt bottle	24	Large Shrimp, peeled, tails on
			Oil for deep frying

Lay won ton wrappers on a table. Place one leaf of basil on each. Place one shrimp on each piece of basil. Roll won ton closed around shrimp. Deep fry at 350 degrees until won ton becomes crisp and shrimp is lightly cooked, 1½–2 minutes. Arrange shrimp on a plate. Ladle some sweet and sour sauce over. Place a spoon full of Hawaiian salsa on shrimp. Finish by squirting some Hoisin sauce over the shrimp and plate. Serves six.

For Banana Imu Style Fish with a Lemon Grass Pesto and Vanilla Bean Sauce from Pacific 'O, see page 188.

When I walked through the doors of Casa de Mateo, I felt like I was stepping into another place and time. What a remarkable experience. Everything felt very authentic.

The cuisine is based on the Oaxaca region of Mexico, which is southeast of Mexico City. Owners, Mateo and Laurie Madoni and many family members from Oaxaca, assist in the restaurant, adding to the authentic experience. Mateo combines his chef training from Belgium with his background from Oaxaca to create incredible and delicious dishes. I watched as a young woman prepared homemade corn and flour tortillas by hand and served them warm and fresh. She then came to my table to make fresh guacamole. The organic ingredients from Hana were blended together with a pestle and mortar (or "Molcagete", made from volcano rock) until the guacamole was perfect for my taste. All the food there is very fresh. Even the margaritas (which are great!) are made with fresh Maui limes. I ate cactus for the first time, which was served as a tasty appetizer. Entrees include: Pato (duck) Con Mole Verde, unique seafood specialties, and various versions of enchiladas. Be sure to try the smooth and delicious banana or papaya flambé for dessert, prepared at your table.

Mateo says the food they serve is very sensual. I agree. This mysterious quality will entice one to return many times.

Casa de Mateo is located above Pacific'O, and has a spectacular view of the ocean and the island of Lanai. Live music is featured on some evenings. Call for information. Open daily. Lunch and dinner $10.00–$20.00.

Salsa de Chile Pasilla (Pasilla Sauce)

1 Tablespoon	Vegetable Oil	1 Teaspoon	Salt
4	Chile Pasilla deveined and without seeds	⅔ Cup	Water
1	Garlic Clove	1 Tablespoon	White Vinegar
		½ Teaspoon	Dry Oregano

In a sauté pan, heat oil, add chiles and sauté for 40 seconds without tossing. Add garlic, salt, water and sauté slowly. Add pieces of chopped chile, vinegar and oregano. Serve over meats or tortillas.

Pollo en Ajillo

1	3 Pound Chicken, cut in pieces	⅓ Cup	Olive Oil
4	Chilies, seeded and deveined	6	Guajillo Chilies
		4	Garlic Cloves
			Salt

Salt chicken and place in large pot; cover with 4 cups water and boil at medium heat. Cover once it boils, and simmer for 20 minutes or until chicken is tender. Turn pieces only once! Separate. Drain and save 2 cups broth. Soak chilies in hot water for 15 minutes; drain. Blend guajillo chilies in 1 cup cold water and set aside. Blend garlic cloves in ⅓ cup water and set aside. Cut seeded and deveined chilies into ½" strips. In pan with *hot* olive oil add sliced chilies until crisp. Add garlic puree and blended chilies and stir constantly for about 5 minutes or until mixture is reduced and thickened. Beware of sticking! Add chicken broth and heat to simmer. Add chicken pieces to large pot and cover with sauce; cook slowly for 25 minutes, stirring frequently. Serve very hot!

Chez Paul is highly recommended. The atmosphere is charming, intimate, and very romantic. Paintings by Guy Buffet (a well known French artist based on Maui) and Robert Lyn Nelson (also a well known Maui artist) are on the walls, including a portrait of the restaurant by each artist. Photographs of well-known people who have eaten at Chez Paul are fun to check out (Robert Redford, Carol Burnett, Elton John, Chevy Chase, Michael Douglas...).

The service here is very gracious and friendly. They know how to make each guest feel special and enjoy making people laugh. The family feeling of the small staff there is nice to experience.

Lucien, owner and executive chef of Chez Paul, calls himself a "Bon Vivant", which means a person who likes to eat and drink well. The recipes he creates are inspired from traveling around the world.

The food is excellent with incredible flavors. A superb appetizer is the Feuillete aux champignons sauvages (puff pastry filled with wild mushrooms). Their most popular dish (the recipe has been published in Gourmet and Food and Wine magazines) is Poisson des iles au beurre–blanc–fresh island fish poached in champagne, shallots, cream and capers.

Chef Steve Smith (who has been with Chez Paul for eight years) prepared this for my dinner and it is outstanding.

Dinner nightly.

$18.00–$33.00.

Call for reservations.

Poisson Beurre–Blanc—Poached Fish

Court Bouillon

12	Whole Black Peppercorns	3 Sprigs	Tarragon
3	Bay Leaves	3 Sprigs	Fresh Thyme
1½ Cups	White Wine	1	Fillet, cut into medallions
1½ Quarts	Water		

Bring all ingredients except for fish to a boil. Pour through colander into a pot and simmer leftover water for 15 minutes. Discard dry ingredients.

To poach: Keep liquid at a slow simmer. Place fish in liquid for 3–5 minutes depending on thickness. Drain on a towel and place on plate. Cover with sauce (recipe below) and garnish with capers.

Sauce

1½ Cups	White Wine	3	Bay Leaves
1½ Cups	Cream	1 Tablespoon	Shallots, chopped
½ Pound	Salted Butter	2 Ounces	Raspberry Vinegar
1 Pound	Sweet Butter		Salt and Pepper to Taste

Combine bay leaves, shallots, wine and vinegar. Reduce until 1½ tablespoons of liquid remains. Remove bay leaves. Add cream and reduce until it starts to thicken. Over low heat, whisk in vigorously small pieces of butter one by one until all the butter is incorporated. Do not let sauce come to a boil—just melt butter.

Creme Brulee

6	Large Egg Yolks	½	Vanilla Bean, split length-wise
½ Cup	Sugar		
3 Cups	Heavy Cream		

In a double boiler whip the egg yolks and sugar on high heat until the mixture is nice and thick with a lemony color. Take off the heat and whip in the heavy cream and the vanilla bean. Put back on the stove at low heat and stir with a wooden spoon until cream thickens and slightly sticks to the spoon. Mix in fresh fruit if you wish. Let it cool down and refrigerate in rammequin dishes for about 3 hours. To serve, cover the individual rammequins with a large amount of powdered sugar and sprinkle granulated sugar over the top. Put directly under the broiler until golden brown. Add a touch of fresh whipped cream.

Ray and Janie Ennis felt that Kihei needed a fun, friendly place with affordable, high quality, healthy food. Stella Blues (named after a Grateful Dead song) is owned and operated by Ray and Janie, with three other family members. They usually have rock and roll playing and live music is featured Wednesday and Friday (7:00–9:00 p.m.), including a selection of blues, jazz, and a contemporary mix.

They have a great menu with daily specials and homemade soups. They use fresh locally grown produce and offer a fresh fish special daily. Popular breakfast items include: East Coast Scramble (scrambled eggs with Nova Scotia Salmon, grilled onions, home fries and a toasted bagel), Tofu Scramble, and South of the Border. Lunch items: Stella's Special—roasted sweet red peppers, feta cheese, grilled eggplant, sliced cucumber and lettuce greens with chunks of roasted garlic and pesto mayonnaise, served on herb bread. Other favorites include Toby's Tofu Tia Extraordinaire, the Pastrami Melt and Reuben sandwiches.

The Vegetarian Delight and Baby Back Ribs with mango plum sauce are popular dinner items. Stella Blues also offers espresso drinks and delicious homemade desserts and pastries (Ricotta Cheesecake with fruit topping, Two Mousse Cake, Chocolate Eclairs, etc.)

Open daily 8:00 a.m. to 10:00 p.m. Breakfast and lunch $4.50–$8.50. Dinner $10.00–$17.00.

Tofu Scramble with Tahini Sauce

2 Cups	Firm Tofu cut in small pieces		1 Cup	Jack Cheese, shredded
½ Cup	Broccoli Heads, diced		½ Cup	Tahini Sauce (recipe below)
½ Cup	Mushrooms, sliced		2 Tablespoons	Butter
½ Cup	Green Onions, sliced			

Sauté vegetables and tofu in butter. Add Tahini Sauce and toss. Add jack cheese and cook until cheese is melted. Serve hot. Serves two.

Tahini Sauce

1 Cup	Toasted Sesame Tahini		1 Teaspoon	Cumin
¾ Cups	Water		2 Teaspoons	Soy Sauce
1	Lemon, juiced		¼ Cup	Fresh Parsley, minced
3 Cloves	Garlic, minced		Dash	Cayenne

Mix together. Makes 1 cup.

Crab Cakes with Lemon Butter Chive Sauce

1	Shallot, minced		2 Cups	Crab Meat, shredded
3 Tablespoons	Butter		1 Tablespoon	Lemon Juice
2	Beaten Eggs		1 Teaspoon	Fresh Dill, minced
½ Cup	Heavy Cream		½ Teaspoon	Salt
1 Cup	Fresh Bread Crumbs		½ Teaspoon	Paprika

Sauté the shallots in 2 tablespoons of the butter, simmer 3 minutes, reserving 1 tablespoon butter and ½ cup bread crumbs. Combine the remaining ingredients and add the shallots. Chill this mixture two hours.

Shape into six 3" cakes and roll in bread crumbs. Melt 1 tablespoon butter in a sauté pan and quickly brown on both sides. Lower the heat and simmer the cakes slowly about 7 minutes longer. Serves two.

Lemon Butter Chive Sauce

2	Shallots, minced		1 Tablespoon	Lemon Juice
¼ Cup	Butter		¼ Cup	Heavy Cream
½ Cup	Dry White Wine		2 Tablespoons	Chives, finely chopped

Sauté shallots in butter. Stir in other ingredients.
Cover the bottom of the plates with sauce and place 3 cakes per plate.

FIVE PALMS BEACH GRILL
(808) 879–2607 • 2960 South Kihei Rd, Kihei, Maui 96753

The soothing sound of the surf, a soft ocean breeze and a view of the glistening Pacific Ocean create a beautiful and relaxing tropical atmosphere at Five Palms Beach Grill. Opened in the summer of 1994, Five Palms has truly created an incredible place to have a remarkable dining experience for breakfast, lunch, or a romantic sunset dinner.

Executive chef Darren McGraw grew up in what he calls "a restaurant family" and has always loved to cook. He was trained at the California Culinary Academy in San Francisco. His philosophy is to create bold, crisp flavors with an emphasis on fresh ingredients and a lighter, more health conscious cuisine. He enjoys the creativity involved in preparing a special menu nightly. Specialty entrées include: Thai Snapper deep fried whole in an Indonesian Jungle Curry with wok charred vegetables, and Grilled Filet

Mignon over Potato Galette and a spinach salad in a date and brandy reduction (sauce). Lunch entrées include: Chinese Style Grilled Chicken Breast Salad with plum–ginger sesame dressing, and an Open Face Fish Taco. Delicious! Breakfast offers a choice of omeletes, eggs florentine, and macadamia nut pancakes.

They feature a great selection of wines and fabulous desserts! (Darren has experience as a pastry chef.) Try the individual Chocolate Mousse with Basil Creme Anglaise or a Zinfandel Poached Pear Tart in baked Creme D'amande.

Open daily. Breakfast $5.00–$11.00. Lunch $5.00–$12.00. Dinner entrées $11.00–$28.00.

Peanut Dressing

½ Cup	Peanut Butter		¼ Teaspoon	Five Spice Powder
½ Cup	Rice Wine Vinegar		1 Tablespoon	Garlic and Ginger, chopped and sautéed
1 Cup	Soy Sauce			
3 Tablespoons	Honey		2 Tablespoons	Fresh Cilantro
1 Tablespoon	Sesame Oil			

Put the above ingredients into a food processor and blend until smooth. If the consistency is too thick, thin with coffee.

Pan Fried Hawaiian Swordfish, Citrus Risotto, Tahitian Peppercorn, Lemon Grass Cream Sauce

6 Pieces	Swordfish, 7 ounces each		1 Ounce	Olive Oil
½ Ounce	Tahitian Peppercorns			

Crush peppercorn and rub the swordfish on both sides. Sauté the fish in hot olive oil, 4 minutes on each side until medium rare. Keep the pieces aside until the rest of the preparation is ready.

Risotto

1	Lemon		2	Onions, small
1 Pound	Risotto (Italian Specialty Rice)		4 Cups	Chicken Stock
			½ Ounce	Parmesan

Sauté the onion in butter until soft, then add the rice (risotto), sauté for a few more minutes. Incorporate chicken stock a little at a time, cook until tender, about 15 minutes. Then add parmesan cheese, squeeze of lemon and salt and pepper to taste.

Lemon Grass Cream Sauce

3 Ounces	Lemon Grass		¼ Ounce	Butter
4 Pieces	Shallots		1 Cup	Fish Stock
2 Cups	Cream		1 Cup	White Wine

Slice lemon grass and shallots, then sauté in butter until lightly brown. Deglaze with white wine, add cream and stock, reduce, season to taste. Simmer for 10 minutes and strain the sauce in a baine marie. Keep warm. Garnish the entrée with asparagus or any other delicate vegetable.

LOBSTER COVE AND HARRY'S SUSHI BAR

(808) 879–7677 • 100 Ike Drive, Wailea, Maui 96753

Lobster Cove and Harry's Sushi Bar offer you two delightful choices under one roof. On most evenings you will be warmly greeted by Lobster Cove's owner/manager, Guido Hauwaerts. Lobster Cove is lovely, small, open air, and looks out over a serene pond. The incredible food is created by Chef Tom Newcomer. The Sweet and Sour Crispy Shrimp with pineapple salsa is an excellent appetizer. Their Live Maine Lobster gets rave reviews; Dungeness Crab and daily fresh fish specials are also popular. Be sure to check for their dessert selections. Their specialty is a unique variation of apple pie. A different selection of wines is featured by the glass each evening (and are always available by the bottle).

Harry making sushi.

It is great fun to sit at Harry's Sushi Bar (located in Lobster Cove) and engage in the conversation and good humor exchanged between Harry and his customers. Harry was trained in Japan and speaks a few different languages. I sat in a spot where I could see how fast his expert hands move to create delightfully appealing and tasty plates of sushi. Seating at Harry's Sushi Bar is limited and is on a first come, first served basis.

Dinner nightly. Entrees $19.00–$35.00. Sushi $4.00–$15.00. Reservations recommended for Lobster Cove. Located next to the Chart House, shares parking lot and entrance.

"Bird Nest" Lobster Cake with Ginger Wasabi Sauce

1 Pound	Chopped Maine Lobster	1 Teaspoon	Celery Seed
½ Pound	Scallop Puree	1 Teaspoon	Paprika
¼ Pound	Chopped Shrimp	1 Teaspoon	Cayenne Pepper
¼ Cup	Fresh Bread Crumbs	1 Teaspoon	Ground Coriander Seed
⅛ Cup	Chopped Scallions		Salt and Pepper to Taste
1 Cup	Mayonnaise		

Mix all the spices with the bread crumbs. Mix the chopped lobster, shrimp, scallions and mayonnaise with the scallop puree. Combine bread crumb mixture with lobster mixture. Shape into patties and sauté.

Ginger Wasabi Sauce

2 Pounds	Tomatoes	¼ Cup	Wasabi Powder
½ Pound	Pickled Ginger		

Puree the tomatoes, pickled ginger, and wasabi powder together and strain.

Garnish

5	Deep Fried Cappelinni Rounds (Angel Hair Pasta)	1 Cup	Chopped Chives

Pour some sauce on each plate, set fried cappelinni on sauce. Place each patty on the "nest" of cappelinni and garnish with chopped chives.

Saeng's Thai Cuisine is a popular place to enjoy Thai food in a pleasant tropical garden setting in downtown Wailuku. The Lahaina location offers an ocean view and open air atmosphere.

Vilay Douangphoumy and his brothers came to the United States from Laos in 1979. They own and operate the two restaurants offering authentic Thai cooking which they learned from their family—especially their mother. "Only Hawaii provides the fresh aromatic herbs, used in Thai cooking, throughout the year as in Thailand or in the Southeast Asian region." Vilay explains that he uses "lime leaves, lemon grass, basil, mint and ginger," among other fresh ingredients in his cooking.

They have a large menu of great selections and also feature daily specials. Saeng's accommodates a variety of taste buds by offering all dishes with a choice of mild to hot seasonings.

Specially recommended items include: Hot and Sour Spicy Chicken, Seafood or Won Ton Soup, Honey Lemon Chicken, Basil Chicken or Beef, and Lobster Curry. There are many vegetarian choices. Refreshing desserts include Thai Tapioca pudding, Coffee Mud Pies and Cheese Cake. Wailuku location (off of Market Street) serves lunch Monday through

Friday. Dinner nightly. Entrees $7.00–$14.00. Lahaina location open daily for lunch and dinner.

Garlic Fish

7–8 Ounces	Mahi Mahi or other similar fish	½ Teaspoon	Sugar
5 Ounces	Coconut Milk	½ Ounce	Thai Fish Sauce
1 Clove	Chopped Fresh Garlic (or more to taste)	Dash	Salt
			Green Onion, chopped
			Black Pepper to Taste

Grill or fry fish. Fry fresh garlic in hot oil until brown. Pour in coconut milk, add sugar, Thai fish sauce, dash of salt, and black pepper. Place cooked fish on a bed of fresh lettuce, cover with sauce, and garnish with green onion or Chinese parsley.

Thai Fried Chicken

6 Pieces	Chicken Breast or Thigh	3 Dashes	Salt to Taste
½ Stalk	Lemon Grass, finely chopped	½ Ounce	Chili Paste
4	Kaffir Lime Leaves, chopped	One Handful	Flour
			Water

Cut chicken into smaller pieces. Blend all other ingredients together, adding enough water to make a nice consistency for marinating. Marinate chicken for a minimum of 10 minutes, preferably for a few hours. Fry chicken until done.

The five owners of Wunderbar are from Germany. They own eight restaurants in and around Nuremberg, Germany, and take turns overseeing Wunderbar. They have known each other since high school, and originally started out together as a rock and roll band. Wunderbar is a fun place, and features live music three nights a week. Thursday through Saturday you can dance your heart out to hot blues, rock 'n roll, and jazz. Sunday afternoon is a time to enjoy live acoustic music.

The executive chef, Martin Lackner is from Austria. Fresh, organically grown Maui produce, and quality local fresh fish and meat are the base for many of their "wunderful" dishes. A German special is featured each night, as well as fresh fish, and a pasta special. The European cuisine is unique for the islands and attracts a lot of European visitors and residents. Wunderbar offers two German beers on tap— Warsteiner and Spaten, plus a good selection of European bottled beers and wines.

Try one of these for lunch: Schnitzelburger, Nuremburger, or Wunder Burger. Dinner favorites are: Paella Andalusia, and Wunder Pasta— Seafood in white wine, garlic, tomatoes and fresh herbs.

It's a great place to stop for breakfast on your way to Hana or for a cold German beer on your way back!

Breakfast $4.00–$8.00. Lunch $5.00–$12.00. Dinner $13.00–$22.00. Open daily.

Ono Avocado Salad

1	Ripe Avocado, cut in slices	6 Ounces	Ono Fillet (¼" slices), marinated in Lemon Juice, Salt, White Pepper
	Mixed Lettuce (green leaf, Lollo Rosso, Romaine, Butter)	1 Teaspoon	Olive Oil

Vinaigrette Dressing

2 Tablespoons	Olive Oil	1 Tablespoon	Finely Chopped Parsley
1 Tablespoon	Sherry or Red Wine Vinegar	1 Teaspoon	Lemon Juice
1 Tablespoon	Water	½ Teaspoon	Dijon Mustard
1 Tablespoon	Finely Chopped Onions		Minced Garlic, Salt, Brown Pepper to Taste

Put all dressing ingredients in a casserole and boil it briefly. Heat olive oil in a frying pan and lightly sauté the seasoned fish. Place lettuce on a plate, the avocado slices at it's right and left. Put the sautéed Ono on top of the lettuce and top everything with the warm dressing. Serves two.

Stew Casimir

8 Ounces	Fish Fillet or Chicken Breast or Turkey Breast	3 Tablespoons	Spicy Madras Curry
		2 Tablespoons	Flour
2 Ounces	Pineapple	2 Teaspoons	Olive Oil
2 Ounces	Apple	3 Tablespoons	White Wine
2 Ounces	Mango	1 Pint	Whipping Cream
2 Ounces	Papaya		Salt, Brown Pepper,
2 Ounces	Thinly Sliced Onions		Cayenne Pepper to Taste
2 Cloves	Minced Garlic		

Cut the fruit into bite size pieces. Coat fish or meat with a mixture of 2 tablespoons of the curry, the flour, salt, pepper and cayenne pepper. Put olive oil in a frying pan, add onions, garlic, and the rest of the curry powder. Sauté slowly until it gets brown. Add fish or meat and fruits and sauté for 2 minutes. Deglaze it with the wine and add whipping cream. Simmer (not boil!) for 5 minutes. Serve with rice pilaf or steamed rice. Serves two.

MAMA'S FISH HOUSE

(808) 579-8488 • 799 Poho Place, Paia, Maui 96779

Established in 1973, Mama's Fish House was a dream come true for owners Floyd and Doris (Mama) Christenson. They first bought a sail boat and spent a year sailing and learning how to navigate. Then they sailed off to Tahiti and had two kids. They loved it! Their next dream was to own a restaurant. So they came to Maui and created the very popular Mama's Fish House. With a charming Tahitian/Hawaiian atmosphere, Mama's sits right on Kuau Cove and offers "a slice of old Hawaii".

They use lots of fresh fruit, herbs and organic greens. They serve the freshest fish (whatever was caught that morning) with a choice of six delicious preparations. A very popular signature item is the Pua Me Hua Hana—Fresh fish sautéed with banana, fresh tropical fruit (mango, lychee, papaya) and a fresh young coconut. A feast for the eyes and mouth.

I first ate at Mama's 10 years ago. It was highly recommended in the community and it still is!

Lunch $8.00–$22.00. Dinner entrées $20.00–$46.00. Open daily. They are located just 1 1/2 miles past Paia Town. Watch for their antique vans.

Hana Ginger Salad with Coconut Sautéed Fish

1 **English Cucumber, peeled, seeded, quartered lengthwise, sliced in ½" pieces**	2 **Avocados, ½" cubes, sprinkled with juice from 1 Lime**
1 **Red Bell Pepper, seeded, ½" strips, diagonally cut**	2 **Papayas, peeled, seeded, ½" cubes, sprinkled with Juice from 1 Lime**
½ Cup **Mango Salsa (recipe below)**	

Gently toss and divide on 4 plates of spinach leaves. Serve extra salsa on the side. Serves four.

Mango Salsa

3 **Mangos, minced (1½ Cups)**	4 Tablespoons **Fresh Lime Juice**
2 Tablespoons **Minced Ginger**	2 Tablespoons **Brown Sugar**
2 Tablespoons **Minced Cilantro**	1 Tablespoon **Sweet Chinese Chili Sauce**
	4 **Green Onions, sliced thin**

Mix all ingredients together.

Coconut Fish

4 **6–8 Ounce Pieces of Fish (mild, light textured)**	1 Teaspoon **Curry Powder**
1 Cup **Sweetened Flaked Coconut**	2 Teaspoons **Lemon Peel, grated**
1 Cup **Panko (Japanese Flour Meal)**	2 Teaspoons **Lime Peel, grated**
	All Purpose Flour
1 Teaspoon **Ground Ginger**	1 Egg **Beaten with 2 Tablespoons Water**
	3 Tablespoons **Vegetable Oil**

Combine coconut, panko, ginger, curry, lemon and lime peel. Rinse fish, pat dry and dust lightly with flour. Dip fish into egg mixture, drain briefly then turn in coconut mixture to coat. Heat oil in a wide frying pan. Add fish and cook turning once—about 6 minutes total.

For Kuau Mahi Sauté from Mama's Fish House, see page 189.

MAKAWAO STEAK HOUSE

(808) 572–8711 • 3612 Baldwin Ave., Makawao, Maui 96768

A friend took me to the Makawao Steak House and said, "They have the best calamari you've ever tasted." So I tried it. He was right. Their Calamari Strips appetizer is outstanding.

They are located in a quaint old house built in 1927. The house has many rooms which create different dining areas, including a comfortable lounge with a fireplace. The walls are decorated with original paintings by local artists. Owners Dickie and Judy Furtado enjoy being a part of the neighborhood community and offer something for everyone. They say, "We're about good food, good cheer, families, celebrations, good times, and great service." They have created a comfortable meeting place that a diverse group of people can enjoy. In their desire to serve the community they offer the full menu selection in the lounge, as well as sandwiches (like Prime Rib) and light specials (only $6.75).

Some of the dinner favorites include: Fresh Fish, Prime Rib, Pork Chop Rosemary, and their Porterhouse Steak. They have delicious dessert selections of which their incredible mud pie is the most popular.

Dinner nightly. Full dinners $16.25–$28.00.

Chicken Zoie

3 Pounds	Frozen Spinach, thawed and drained well	1 Pound	Finely Chopped Ham
4	Green Onions with tops finely chopped	1½ Cups	White Wine
		6	Boneless, Skinless Chicken Breasts

Sauce

½ Pound	Butter	2	Bay Leaves
1 Cup	Flour	½ Teaspoon	Salt
3 Cups	Milk	1 Teaspoon	Black Pepper

Sauté ham and green onion. Add wine, reduce until liquid is almost gone, add spinach and sauté until liquid is almost gone. Set aside.

To make sauce, blend butter, flour, and milk, slowly whisk and cook until smooth. Add bay leaves, salt and pepper. Combine this with the spinach mixture. Spoon mixture into chicken breasts and fold seam side down on baking sheet. Bake in 400 degree oven until tender and barely cooked.

Dynamite

1	Large Zucchini, julienne	1½ Pounds	Scallops
1	Large Onion, julienne	½ Pound	Crab Meat, shredded

Sauce

1½ Cups	Mayonnaise		Bread Crumbs to cover
1 Tablespoon	Tabasco		Parmesan Cheese sprinkled over all
2 Tablespoons	Chili Powder		

Sauté zucchini and onion in butter until limp. Drain on paper towels. Let sit for 1 hour and squeeze excess liquid with paper towels. Toss the mixture with the scallops and crab meat. Spoon into *shallow* oven proof dishes. Mix the mayonnaise, Tabasco, and chili powder together and spoon over the seafood mixture. Sprinkle liberally with bread crumbs and top with parmesan. Broil until browned and bubbly—5 to 7 minutes. Serve with crusty French bread. Serves 8–10 as an appetizer.

Cynthia Burke, owner of the The Courtyard Deli, is doing her dream. She has created a comfortable, warm and friendly place that is a home away from home for many. Cynthia says her food is "made from the heart, using the freshest ingredients to create a dish that's pleasing, beautiful, and has a good feeling." It's also healthy and tastes great!

Cynthia believes that simple pleasures are what we need when everything else in our lives gets crazy. On her commute to work, instead of sitting in traffic, she has seen four baby cows being born! How's that for simple pleasures?

The Courtyard Deli was voted Best Deli on Maui by the Maui News Reader's Survey. Local musicians stop by to play in the shady, quaint open courtyard. Sitting inside is also pleasant, and gives you a chance to admire and choose from the beautiful display of gourmet chocolate candies, and a wide assortment of delicious and tempting homemade pastries and desserts (Mango pie, Strawberry Rhubarb pie, Carrot Cake, muffins, cookies, etc.). They are perfect with an espresso or cappuccino.

Breakfast favorites include Claire's Cinnamon Custard French Toast and Cindi's Tofu Scramble. For lunch—Polenta Lasagna Casserole or a fresh ground Ahi burger made with fresh herbs and spices. Unique daily specials, sandwiches, homemade soups, and salads are also featured.

Breakfast and lunch daily $3.00 to well under $10.00.

Flaky Buttermilk Scones

7½ Cups	Flour	1⅛ Cups	Butter or Soy Margarine
1 Tablespoon	Baking Soda	2¾ Cups	Buttermilk
1 Tablespoon	Baking Powder		Cinnamon/Sugar Mixture
1 Teaspoon	Salt		

Optional—Choice of Frozen Blueberries, Raisins, Walnuts, Chopped Candied Ginger. Should be mixed in prior to adding Buttermilk.

Sift dry ingredients together in large mixing bowl. Cut butter/margarine into small pieces and basically rub into flour mixture until mixture is slightly crumbly. Make a small well in the center of the flour/butter mixture and stir in buttermilk. Turn mixture out onto a floured board and knead gently. Excessive kneading creates a tough scone. Leave small chunks of butter, small pea size, throughout and knead the dough just enough to form into two rounds. When baking, the butter chunks melt, creating a flakier scone. When forming the two rounds, make the center slightly higher, creating a mound effect. Cut each round into 6 triangular shapes, sprinkle with cinnamon/sugar mixture and bake at 400 degrees for 15–20 minutes. While still hot, slice in half and fill with your favorite jam. Serve toasty hot. Makes one dozen extra large scones.

Courtyard Frittata

1 Bunch	Fresh Spinach or 1–2 Cups Frozen Spinach thawed and drained	2 Cups	Grated Cheese (one or a mixture of several)
¼ Pound	Sliced Mushrooms	12	Eggs
2 Medium	Tomatoes, chopped	1¼ Cups	Buttermilk Baking Mix
½ Cup	Sliced Green Onions (with tops)		Salt and Pepper or Spike and Cayenne to Taste
(Optional) 1	Red Pepper, diced	¼ Teaspoon	Oregano, Basil or your Favorite Herb

If using fresh spinach, wash, chop and steam slightly retaining bright green color. Drain and place in bottom of 13" X 9" X 2" greased baking dish. If using frozen spinach, thaw, drain and place in dish as above. Continue layering mushrooms, tomatoes, onions, pepper and cheese. Beat remaining ingredients together and pour over vegetable mixture. Bake uncovered in 350 degree oven until golden brown and set, about 30 minutes. Cut and serve with Buttermilk Scones and fresh fruit.

The little town of Makawao is on the map when it comes to good food! It used to be primarily a paniolo (cowboy) town. But in the last several years, it has grown into an inviting and charming place to browse through art galleries, shops, and enjoy great food.

Polli's was voted #1 for Best Mexican Food on Maui by the Maui News reader's poll. It was established in 1981 and is now owned by brothers Tim and Chris Ellison. Their first jobs were as waiters at Sid's Delicatessen in the U.S. Virgin Islands, where the sign out front read, "COME IN AND EAT OR WE'LL BOTH STARVE!" Tim stayed in the restaurant business while Chris became an airline pilot.

Polli's offers a diverse menu and includes non-Mexican items such as hamburgers, grilled chicken sandwiches, BBQ Chicken, and Baby Back Ribs. Popular Mexican items include Seafood Enchiladas, Sizzling Fajitas and Burritos Supreme—you can choose a filling of Seafood, Chicken, Beef, Vegetarian or Chile Relleno. There are great desserts to choose from and, of course, Margaritas!

Tim and Chris "are committed to continuing the tradition of good food and good service, at reasonable prices, and all with the Aloha spirit."

Lunch $5.50–$12.00. Dinner $6.50–$16.00.

Open daily.

Guacamole

10 Pounds	Ripe Avocados	½ Teaspoon	Garlic Powder
¼ Cup	Diced Onions	1 Teaspoon	Lemon Juice
½ Cup	Sour Cream	1 Teaspoon	Salt
1 Tablespoon	Finely Chopped Jalapeños		

Cut avocados in half. Remove the seed. Spoon out into a bowl, remove all brown spots. Mash. Add all other ingredients. Mix thoroughly until smooth. Leave three avocado seeds at the bottom of the container to maintain freshness and reduce browning. Makes 20 servings.

Salsa

9 Cups	Diced Tomatoes	½ Teaspoon	Red Wine Vinegar
⅔ Cup	Diced Green Chilies	¾ Cup	Finely Chopped Jalapeños
2 Cups	Tomato Sauce	½ Teaspoon	Cilantro
3⅓ Cups	Diced Green Onions	1 Teaspoon	Salt
2 Cloves	Garlic		

In a food processor, mix soft tomatoes, green onions, garlic, and cilantro. Add remaining ingredients and mix thoroughly. Makes one gallon.

Polli's Vegetarian Chili

5 Tablespoons	Butter	½ Teaspoon	Cayenne Pepper
1 Cup	Diced Onions	4 Cups	Cooked Beans
1 Cup	Bell Peppers, finely chopped	2 Cups	Bean Juice
		3 Cups	Whole Tomatoes
1½ Teaspoons	Cumin	½ Teaspoon	Salt, or to Taste
6 Tablespoons	Chili Powder	1 Cup	Tomato Sauce
¾ Teaspoon	Garlic Powder		

Sauté onions and bell peppers in butter, Add remaining ingredients. Mix well and simmer in an uncovered pot over low heat for one hour.

CASANOVA ITALIAN RESTAURANT

(808) 572–0220 • 1188 Makawao Ave., Makawao, Maui 96768

Casanova is a favorite place for the Upcountry community to enjoy great authentic Italian food as well as fabulous entertainment. It all began with the small Gourmet Deli next door, which the 3 Italian owners opened in 1986. It was so successful, that when the opportunity arose in 1989, Casanova expanded into the larger space next door to create a fine dining restaurant as well. Twice the Maui News Readers Survey voted Casanova "Best Italian Restaurant" and "Best Pizza" on Maui. The Zagat Survey called them "Best Food and Entertainment Combo" on the island.

Pizzas are baked to perfection in a real wood burning oven. Fresh pastas are made from scratch, like the delicious Ravioli filled with Smoked Salmon, soft cheese and dill. Seafood is offered in creative preparations like Penne Pasta with Lobster in sherry sauce. The Fresh Fish is baked whole with white wine and fresh herbs, and there are many tempting vegetarian choices.

Casanova was a famous Italian lover in the 1700's known for his amorous adventures and for the dessert, Tiramisu, or Italian love cake, which legend says he created to "revive himself after his bedtime battles". You can taste the sublime Tiramisu at Casanova Restaurant. When dining comes to an end, Casanova lights up as a "top class entertainment club". It features "the largest dance floor on Maui", DJs on Wednesday and Thursday, and live music Friday and Saturday. Casanova has attracted well known performers such as Willie Nelson, Acoustic Alchemy, Taj Mahal, Kool & The Gang, and the late Sam Kinison. Call to see who's scheduled for this week. Deli open daily 8:00a.m.–6:00 p.m. Restaurant open Monday through Saturday. Lunch under $10.00. Dinner entrées $10.00–$23.00.

Gnocchi Strozzapreti al Gorgonzola

2 Pounds	Ricotta Cheese	2 Ounces	Grated Parmesan Cheese
2	Eggs	1½ Ounces	White Flour
8 Ounces	Chopped Spinach (frozen will work, but drain well after defrosting)	1 Teaspoon	Nutmeg
		1 Large Spoonful	Rock Salt
			Parsley

In a bowl, mix by hand, ricotta cheese, eggs, chopped spinach, parmesan cheese, flour, and nutmeg. Mix until ingredients create a soft dough. Roll the dough in a strip of 1" diameter, then cut the strip at 2" intervals. Set aside the dumplings and sprinkle them with white flour. Meanwhile, bring 1 gallon of water to a boil, to which you will add 1 large spoonful of rock salt at boiling time. When the water is boiling, add the dumplings to it. When they start floating, remove them with a strainer and set them on serving platters. Six per person is a generous portion. Pour the gorgonzola sauce on them (recipe below), sprinkle on some chopped parsley, and serve hot.

Gorgonzola Sauce

1 Quart	Cream	8 Ounces	Crumbled Gorgonzola (Blue Cheese is acceptable but delivers a stronger flavor)

In a pan, bring the cream to a boil. When boiling, add gorgonzola cheese. Let it simmer for a few minutes to reach the desired thickness. Help the cheese melt in the cream by stirring with a wooden spoon. Pour the hot sauce onto the dumplings.

For Maccheroni al Ragu D'Agnello (Short Pasta in Lamb Meat Sauce) from Casanova, see page 190.

The Upcountry Cafe is such a fun place! It's charming, country style shows a sense of humor with a very prevalent cow theme which was inspired by the many cows in the upcountry area. There are cow booths outside, cows that pour cream, cow salt and pepper shakers, and pictures of cows that have "Eat Chicken" written underneath. Cows are everywhere! They offer a delectable cow pie for dessert! You'll have to try it to satisfy your curiosity. It's much tastier than it sounds!

The popular Upcountry Cafe opened in 1990. The comfortable, friendly atmosphere, and varied menu, offers something for people of all types and ages. They serve homemade jams, chutneys, guava butter, etc., which are also available by the jar and are great to take home.

For breakfast the Belgian Waffle with fruit is delicious. The Loco Moo−Co and Vegetarian Fritatta are also popular. Lunch offers an award winning Hamburger and other sandwiches. Vegetarian Lasagna, Saimin, great salads, and homemade soups (Portuguese bean, carrot and ginger bisque, clam chowder, etc.) are offered for both lunch and dinner. And you can't beat the price for the fresh island fish served here for dinner.

Breakfast daily, except Tuesday. $2.50−$6.25. Lunch, Monday, Wednesday through Saturday. $4.00−$7.50. Dinner Thursday through Saturday. $7.00−$11.00.

Cheese Crusted Porkloin

1½ Pounds	**Boneless Porkloin**		**Salt and Pepper**
	Granulated Garlic		

Cheese Crust

1 Cup	**Fresh Whole Wheat Bread Crumbs**	**2 Tablespoons**	**Macadamia Nuts, diced**
½ Cup	**Parmesan Cheese, grated**	**1 Tablespoon**	**Fresh Parsley, minced**
½ Cup	**Swiss Cheese, grated**	**¼ Cup**	**Melted Butter**
		2 Cups	**Brown Sauce or Gravy**

Preheat oven to 400 degrees. Rub porkloin with desired amount of salt, pepper, and garlic. Roast in oven for 40–50 minutes until done. Let stand for 10 minutes. Combine remaining ingredients, except brown sauce in a bowl. Heat broiler oven to medium to high heat. Slice pork, place onto pan in layers. Sprinkle cheese mixture evenly over pork. Place pan under broiler until golden brown. Pour heated brown sauce onto serving platter. Place cheese crusted pork over sauce.

Steamed Clams with Sake and Ginger

1 Pound	**Fresh Buttercup or Manila Clams, rinsed well**	**2 Teaspoons**	**Fresh Ginger, grated**
¼ Cup	**Japanese Sake**	**2 Teaspoons**	**Peanut Oil**
2 Tablespoons	**Water**		**Green Onions, sliced for garnish**
2 Tablespoons	**Whole Butter**		

Heat peanut oil in wok or sauté pan. Add ginger, stir for 10 seconds. Add clams, sake, water, and butter. Cover pan and let steam until clams open. Pour into serving bowl, discard unopened clams. Garnish with green onions.

On the scenic slopes of Maui's Haleakala crater, you will find the Kula Lodge and Restaurant nestled in the trees and rolling hills at the 3,200 foot level.

The lodge offers expansive views of Maui and the Pacific Ocean. It is surrounded by a beautiful private garden with a spectacular terrace, which is often used for weddings and private parties. Hundreds of different varieties of protea, trees and flowers are grown there along with fresh herbs used in the restaurant. Other fresh organic produce is supplied by local farmers.

Kula Lodge offers a "feast for your eyes" and also a "feast for your palate". Chef Yannick Gaudey, along with owner, Fred Romanchak, offer the "best in the traditional cuisine" as well as a healthier "upcountry island fare". Two breakfast favorites are Eggs Benedict and Tofu Vegetable Scramble. Lunches offer sandwiches, burgers and items such as Papaya Shrimp Salad. Dinners (also available at lunch time) include Roasted Rack of Lamb, fresh island fish, which is served in a different preparation daily, vegetarian specials, and more.

Other features include the Curtis Wilson Cost Art Gallery and the Hawaii Protea Gift Shop. There are five rustic chalets available for overnight accommodations. It is a perfect place to wake up early for a journey to see the sunrise on Haleakala. Call for more information. Open daily. Breakfast $4.00–$8.00. Lunch salads and sandwiches $6.50–$9.00. Lunch and dinner entrées $12.00–$21.00.

Baked Cucumbers Stuffed with Opakapaka Mousse

3	Cucumbers	1 Cup	Heavy Cream
16 Ounces	Fresh Opakapaka	1 Tablespoon	Macadamia Nuts
2	Egg Whites	2 Tablespoons	Melted Butter
½ Teaspoon	Salt	1 Cup	Beurre Blanc (recipe below)
½ Teaspoon	Paprika		
	Cayenne Pepper		

Cut cucumbers into 1¼" pieces. Scoop out the seeds with a small melon ball cutter. Blanch in boiling salted water for 2 minutes and submerge in ice water. Drain well on a paper towel. In a food processor, puree the opakapaka and add egg whites, salt, cayenne pepper, and paprika. Pour in the heavy cream slowly and the macadamia nuts until well mixed. Place the cucumber cup in a buttered baking dish. Preheat oven to 350 degrees. Fill cucumbers with the opakapaka mousse. Bake for 20 minutes. Place the cucumbers in a serving dish and serve with beurre blanc.

Beurre Blanc

4	Shallots, chopped	1½ Cups	Unsalted Butter, cut into small chunks
3 Tablespoons	White Vinegar		Salt and Ground White Pepper to Taste
1 Cup	White Wine		

Combine shallots, vinegar, and wine in a non–reactive saucepan. Bring to a boil and cook until liquid reduces to 2 tablespoons. Reduce heat to low and whisk in butter, a few chunks at a time until all of the butter has been incorporated. Season with salt and white pepper to taste.

Fresh Spinach with Skillet Roasted Salmon

	Black Peppercorns	2 Tablespoons	Sesame Oil
8 Ounces	Salmon	1 Pound	Fresh Spinach
6 Tablespoons	Unsalted Butter		Coarse Sea Salt

Press black peppercorns into salmon filet. Heat butter and oil in a skillet over medium heat. Add salmon fillets, skin side down, and cook without turning for about 15 minutes. Melt butter in a pot. Add spinach and sprinkle with salt and pepper. Cook the spinach over medium high heat for a few minutes until liquid in skillet evaporates. Place spinach on a serving platter and salmon on the top of the spinach, skin side down. Sprinkle salmon with coarse sea salt and serve.

Grandma's is warm, charming and quaint, just as one would expect it to be. It is fitting for the little town of Keokea where it is located.

Alfred Franco (Grandma's grandson) was inspired by the many generations in his family that have grown and processed coffee on Maui. He was especially inspired by his grandmother, who is now in her 90s. "Grandma taught me how to grow, harvest, process, and drink coffee," he says.

In 1983 Alfred started Grandma's Maui Coffee, and in 1988 he expanded to open Grandma's Coffee House. Both are named in her honor. She gave him her blessing to continue with the family tradition. The coffee is organically grown on Maui. It is processed and roasted using an 1885 roasting machine that has been used in the family for many, many years. The coffee beans are also used to make Grandma's chocolates. Grandma's fresh roasted coffee can be enjoyed in many different forms: iced or hot cappuccino, espresso, latte, or mocha. They serve a variety of fresh baked goods including their delicious coffee cake, fruit cobblers and muffins. Sandwiches, chili and rice, saimin, salads and daily specials are also available. Under $6.00.

Open daily from 7:00 a.m. to middle or late afternoon.

Susan's Hawaiian Chicken Curry Stew

5 Pounds	Boneless, Skinless Chicken Thighs	2 Tablespoons	Curry Powder
3 Cups	Cubed Cut Maui Kula Onions	2 Ounces	Fresh Hawaiian Ginger, chopped
3 Cups	Cut Carrots	1	Whole Clove Garlic, chopped
3 Cups	Potatoes, peeled and cubed	8 Cups	Water
1½ Cups	Chopped Green Bell Pepper	3 Tablespoons	Flour, to thicken gravy
		3 Teaspoons	Ground Black Pepper or to Taste
1½ Cups	Chopped Celery	3 Teaspoons	Sea Salt, or to Taste

Slice chicken thighs into thirds, sauté to brown, then add seasonings including ginger and garlic. Add potatoes, carrots, and water. Simmer over moderate heat for 35 minutes. Then add the rest of the vegetables and simmer for approximately 10 more minutes. Note that all measurements are approximate and may be adjusted to taste.

Maui Lava Flows

Crust

¾ Cup	Unsalted Butter	1 Cup	Packed Maui Raw Sugar
2 Cups	Unbleached Flour		

Mix for approximately 2 minutes. Spread over lightly greased 9" X 13" pan. Bake at 350 degrees for 20–25 minutes until dark brown.

Filling

1½ Cups	Packed Maui Raw Sugar	2 Teaspoons	Pure Vanilla
4	Eggs	2 Cups	Chocolate Chips
4 Tablespoons	Unbleached Flour	1½ Cups	Chopped Pecans
2 Teaspoons	Salt		

Blend all ingredients (except chocolate chips and pecans) in mixer until light and fluffy. Add chocolate chips and pecans, and mix 1 minute. Pour over crust. Bake at 350 degrees 20–25 minutes.

Frosting

3 Tablespoons	Unsalted Butter	1 Teaspoon	Grandma's Maui Coffee Espresso
4 Tablespoons	Cocoa		
4 Tablespoons	Water	2 Cups	Powdered Sugar

Mix first 4 ingredients in sauce pan over medium heat. Bring to a boil and put in mixer. Add sugar and beat until smooth and thick. Drizzle over bars to look like lava flows.

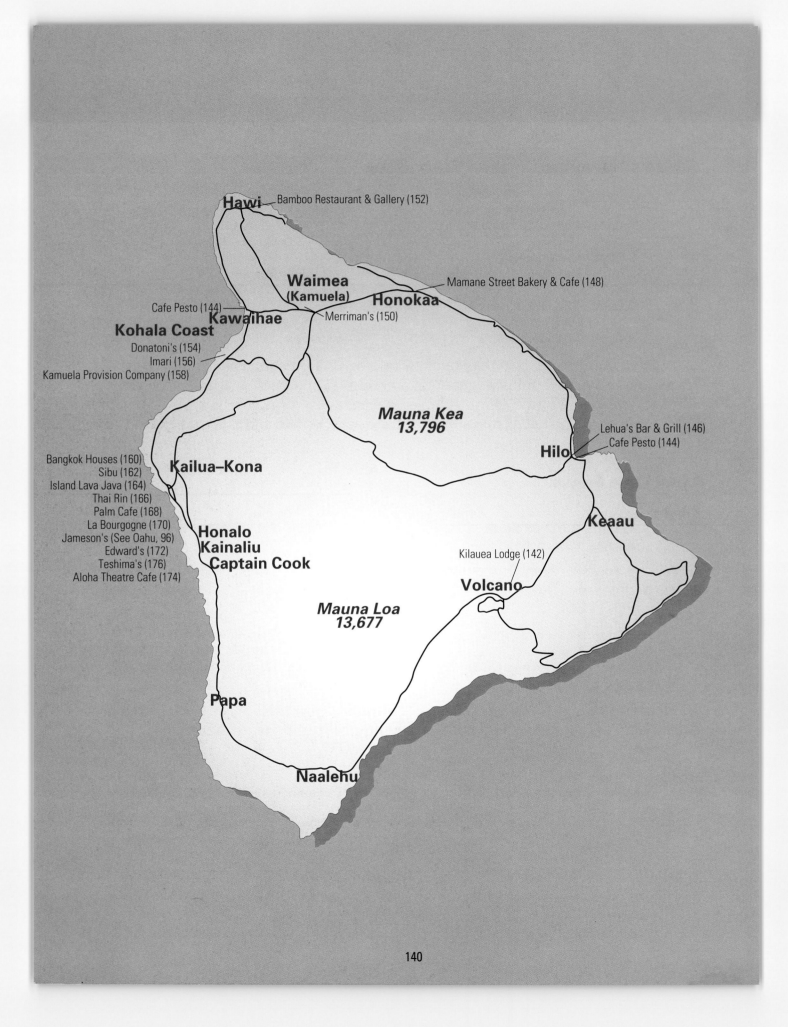

Hawi — Bamboo Restaurant & Gallery (152)

Waimea
(Kamuela)

Honokaa — Mamane Street Bakery & Cafe (148)

Cafe Pesto (144)

Kawaihae — Merriman's (150)

Kohala Coast

Donatoni's (154)
Imari (156)
Kamuela Provision Company (158)

Mauna Kea
13,796

Lehua's Bar & Grill (146)
Cafe Pesto (144)

Hilo

Bangkok Houses (160)
Sibu (162)
Island Lava Java (164)
Thai Rin (166)
Palm Cafe (168)
La Bourgogne (170)
Jameson's (See Oahu, 96)
Edward's (172)
Teshima's (176)
Aloha Theatre Cafe (174)

Kailua–Kona

Keaau

Honalo
Kainaliu
Captain Cook

Kilauea Lodge (142)

Volcano

Mauna Loa
13,677

Papa

Naalehu

Hawaii
The Big Island

Cuisines Featured

The historic "International Fireplace of Friendship" in Kilauea Lodge has been a meeting place for people from all over the world for many years. The lodge was built in 1938 for the YMCA. Over the years, thousands of children on exploration trips to the volcano have stayed there. Inspired by the Volcano during the day, they spent their evenings telling Pele myths by the warm fire.

The buildings were refurbished in 1986 when Lorna and Albert Jeyte bought the lodge. They now offer romantic overnight accommodations which include a complimentary full breakfast .

With lots of wood, fresh flowers, and beautiful original watercolors painted on silk, Kilauea Lodge offers a warm and charming atmosphere for enjoying one of their fabulous dinner entrées or nightly specials.

They always have at least 3 delicious preparations for the fresh catch of the day: sautéed with piccata sauce, broiled with papaya-mango-ginger sauce, or blackened with Hawaiian salsa and candied ginger. They offer vegetable, fowl, and beef selections as well. Dinner nightly $13.00–$27.00. Call for reservations. Located one mile from Volcanoes National Park in Volcano Village.

The beautiful and inviting entrance to Kilauea Lodge.

Cream of Celery Soup

10 Cups	Chicken Broth		1 Cup	Heavy Cream
3 Pounds	Celery Stalk—cubed		1½ Teaspoons	Celery Salt
2 Pounds	Russet Potatoes—peeled and cubed		1 Teaspoon	White Pepper
			8 Ounces	Unsalted Butter
17 Fluid Ounces	Milk			Parsley—finely chopped

Pour chicken stock into 4 quart pot. Bring to a boil. Puree celery and potato in food processor until very fine. Add puree into boiling chicken broth and beat with whip for 2 minutes. Add milk and heavy cream. Stir. Bring to a fast boil, then reduce heat to low and let simmer. Add celery salt and white pepper. Stir. Cover pot and let simmer for 40 minutes. Stir frequently. Remove pot from stove. With a 2 ounce ladle force liquid through a fine sieve into a 4 quart bowl. Discard heavy puree in sieve. Cut butter into ½ inch cubes. Add to cream of celery in the bowl. Whip until butter has dissolved. Sprinkle a little parsley on each serving. Serve cold or hot. For 8–10 people.

Beef Roulades

8–10 Slices	Top Round Beef (Each ¼" thick)		1 Cup	Diced Onion
	Dijon Mustard		4 Ounces	Bacon Fat
	Salt		2 Quarts	Water
	Black Ground Pepper		4 Teaspoons	Cornstarch
1 Cup	Diced Bacon		2 Tablespoons	Cold Water for Cornstarch
3 Spears	Dill Pickle, diced			Toothpicks

Lay out the slices of beef on a table or large cutting board and pound lightly with mallet. Sprinkle with salt and black pepper and spread a little mustard. Add teaspoon each of diced onion, bacon, and dill pickle. Fold in on both sides and roll up tightly. Push in 2 toothpicks. Put aside until all slices are done.

Heat up bacon fat in large enough pot to hold the roulades on the bottom plus 2 quarts of water. Add the roulades and brown on all sides. After browning, add one pint of water slowly from the side first. Add additional water to cover the roulades just to the top. Cover with lid and simmer for 1½–2 hours. Roulades should be soft. Replace water as needed. When roulades are soft, remove and place on a plate.

In a small bowl mix water with cornstarch. Add to simmering sauce and let thicken. Stir. Add roulades again and simmer for 5 more minutes. Stir. Remove toothpicks and serve. Serves four.

Provocative is such a perfect word to describe the intriguing food and atmosphere of Cafe Pesto. "Pizza, pasta, pesto, provocative" is written on their menu—and what an incredible menu! It is full of many deliciously unique and fresh selections. Try Baked Puna Goat Cheese—Sesame crusted with grilled eggplant, spinach, vine ripened tomatoes and basil aioli, for an appetizer, or a Wood Fired Pizza with combinations such as wild mushrooms, artichokes and rosemary gorgonzola sauce.

Their selections of pastas, risottos and calzones are equally unique and delicious, and I couldn't resist their fabulous desserts. I had Ganache—chocolate torte with raspberry puree and vanilla cream swirled over the top. It was sublime.

The atmosphere is fun and lively—a great place for stimulating conversation as well as taste buds! They have been written about in Food & Wine Magazine, and recipes have been requested by Gourmet Magazine. Cafe Pesto is located in the renovated S. Hata Building in historic downtown Hilo at Hilo Bay, and at the Kawaihae Shopping Center, ocean side, lower level. Lunch and dinner, daily. $6.00–$15.00.

Poisson Cru with Tropical Fruits Served Over Baby Greens Dressed with an Ohelo Berry Vinaigrette

1 Pound	Ono (Wahoo) or any White Fish		2 Dashes	Chipolte Vinegar (Tobasco)
½ Cup	Lime Juice		1	Papaya, cubed
1	12 Ounce Can Coconut Milk		2	Bananas, cut in chunks
1	Mango, cubed		2	Kiwi, cut in chunks
				Salad Greens

Cut fish in 1 inch cubes and marinate in lime juice for 1 hour. Drain fish and combine all ingredients and let stand for ½ hour.

Ohelo Berry Vinaigrette

½ Cup	Ohelo Berry Jam*		¼ Teaspoon	Fresh Cracked Pepper
⅓ Cup	Red Wine Vinegar		1 Cup	Oil
1 Tablespoon	Sugar			Salt to Taste
1 Teaspoon	Minced Ginger			

*Use fresh Ohelo berries cooked and thickened with cornstarch.

In a food processor, combine all ingredients except oil. With machine running, add oil slowly.

Lumpia Wrapped Ahi with Fresh Mango

8	2 Ounce Slices of Sashimi Grade Ahi		1 Tablespoon	Wasabi Paste (thinned)
1	Fresh Mango, peeled and sliced thin		2 Sheets	Nori (cut into 8 strips)
				Salt and Pepper
			8	Lumpia (Egg Roll) Shells

Very lightly baste the top of the Ahi with wasabi. Place a slice of fresh mango on the Ahi. Sprinkle lightly with salt and pepper. Wrap the Ahi and mango with a strip of dampened Nori. Place wrapped Ahi in Lumpia shell and fold into a square. Preheat well–oiled sauté pan at medium–high. Sear Ahi Lumpia until golden brown. Damp off any extra oil and cut Lumpias diagonally for presentation. May be served with a mango chutney thinned with rice wine vinegar and spiced with Hawaiian chilies.

One of the fun things about Lehua's is reading the old signs that are hanging all around. They are from businesses that have prospered in Hilo and other places on the Big Island since the turn of the century. I had a clear view of a large sign that said:

Ya gotta have a sense of humor!

Lehua's is located in the historic Hilo Drug Store. The old soda fountain area is still in use and now makes a great bar for Lehua's.

All of the soups, sauces, dressings, salsas and desserts are homemade. I enjoyed the best Cream of Spinach soup I've ever tasted—so smooth and flavorful. Specialties include fresh fish selections, their Deep Dish Cheese pie, and a wonderful Spinach Lasagna—baked with fresh herbs, mushrooms, onions, and four cheeses, with a mild marinara sauce. Delicious!

They often have dancing and live music in the evenings. Lunch $6.00–$11.00. Dinner $8.00–$20.00. Open daily.

Olive, Anchovy, and Caper Tapenade

6	Garlic Cloves	4½ Cups	Pitted Kalamata Olives
3 Ounces	Well Drained Flat Anchovy Fillets (about 18 fillets)	1½ Teaspoons	Dried Rosemary, Crumbled
9 Tablespoons	Well Drained Bottled Capers	1½ Teaspoons	Dried Oregano, crumbled
		¾ Cup	Olive Oil

In a food processor or blender combine all the ingredients, plus salt and pepper to taste and pulse the mixture until coarsely ground. Transfer the Tapenade to a serving dish and present it with crisply toasted sourdough bread or crackers. Yield: about 3 cups.

Fresh Ono with Potato Crust and Roasted Sweet Pepper Sauce

4	Fresh Fish Fillets (6 to 8 ounces each)	½ Teaspoon	Black Pepper
4 Teaspoons	Dijon Mustard	2	Large Raw Potatoes, peeled & coarsely grated
2 Teaspoons	Creole Seasoning (any name brand)	2 Cups	Roasted Sweet Pepper Sauce (see recipe below)
¼ Cup	Olive Oil	½ Cup	Fresh Chives, finely chopped
1 Teaspoon	Salt		

Spread top of each fish fillet with mustard and sprinkle with Creole seasoning. Firmly top each fish fillet with ½ cup grated potatoes and sprinkle with a dash of salt and pepper. Heat olive oil in a non-stick skillet over high heat until hot. Carefully slide fillets into the skillet crust side up and fry 2 to 3 minutes. Turn quickly, crust side down, and fry until dark golden brown, about 2 to 3 minutes. Cover the bottom of dinner plates with pepper sauce and place the fish fillet crusted side up in the center of the sauce. Sprinkle with chives and serve. Yield: 4 servings.

Sweet Pepper Sauce

2 Tablespoons	Olive Oil	1 Teaspoon	Chopped Fresh Basil
3	Medium–Large Red or Yellow Roasted Bell Peppers	1 Teaspoon	Salt
		2 Tablespoons	Heavy Cream
¼ Cup	Chopped Onion	Dash	Cayenne Pepper to Taste
2 Teaspoons	Minced Garlic		Black Pepper to Taste
		2 Cups	Chicken Stock or Broth

To roast the peppers, hold over a stove burner on high heat with a long fork, turning to char evenly. Put into ice water, then peel off skins. Combine oil, peppers, onions, garlic, basil, salt, cayenne and black pepper in a saucepan over high heat and cook for 3 minutes. Stir in chicken stock and cream and bring to a boil. Reduce heat to simmer and stir about 8 minutes. Puree in a blender for 2 minutes and serve while hot.

At 2:00 a.m. the bakers of Mamane Street Bakery & Cafe begin preparing the enticing and delicious pastries, breads, and desserts, for the day. Everything is fresh everyday. Ely Pessah, owner and pastry chef, is originally from Cairo, Egypt. He came to the United States in 1968 and has worked for many years as a pastry chef in four and five star resorts. It is very apparent that he cares a lot about quality, and pleasing his customers. I met people from all over the Island who love going to Ely's bakery.

The atmosphere is quaint and charming, with a few small tables to sit and enjoy scrumptious pastries with an espresso, cappuccino, or herb tea.

The Portuguese Sweet Bread and Honey Macadamia Nut Bran Muffins are very popular. Their seasonal fresh fruit tarts and cheesecakes are delicate, delicious, and exquisitely garnished. (Raspberry and Mango when I was there. Mmmm.) They make fabulous Focaccia–Italian herb breads featuring Pesto and three cheeses, Marinara and Mozzarella, and Salami and Cheese. They also have selected sandwiches and ham and cheese croissants.

Be sure to visit the bakery's adjoining gift shop area featuring local artists. The interior workmanship is also a work of art. People stop by to see the many different types of wood (50, including Hawaiian varieties) that are used in the design. Open daily from 7:00 a.m. through the afternoon. Under $10.00.

Macadamia Nut Brownies

8 Ounces	Unsalted Butter		2½ Cups	Flour
8 Ounces	Semisweet Chocolate		1 Tablespoon	Pure Vanilla
4 Cups	Sugar		4 Ounces	Macadamia Nuts
8	Large Eggs			

Preheat oven to 350 degrees. Melt butter on stove on very low heat. Add chocolate and stir until it dissolves and turn heat off. Add sugar and eggs. Stir. Add flour, vanilla and macadamia nuts. Mix well. Pour batter mixture into a 12" X 18" pan greased with butter. Spread evenly. Bake at 350 degrees, 20–30 minutes. Do not over bake—these brownies are moist. Yield: 54 2" X 2" squares.

Honey Nut Bran Muffins

Pan Dressing/Coating

8 Ounces	Unsalted Butter (softened)		½ Cup	Honey
1⅓ Cups	Light Brown Sugar		1 Tablespoon	Pure Vanilla

Mix all ingredients well.

Bran Mix

1 Cup	Vegetable Oil		5 Cups	Bran
3 Large	Eggs		2½ Cups	Flour
1½ Cups	Sugar		3 Cups	Buttermilk
1 Tablespoon	Salt		1 Cup	Raisins
1 Tablespoon	Baking Soda		6 Ounces	Crushed Pineapple
½ Cup	Honey			

Mix in order listed being careful not to stir too much after adding flour.

**Macadamia Nuts, diced,
or Walnuts, chopped**

Grease muffin pans with 1 tablespoon of Pan Dressing Mixture. Add 1 teaspoon of Macadamia Nuts or Walnuts for each muffin and mix well. Using an ice cream scoop, allow ¾ of a scoop of Bran Mixture for each muffin. Bake at 375 degrees for 25–35 minutes. When done turn the muffin pan upside–down and lift up slowly. Yield: 3 dozen muffins.

The phone rang one January day while Peter Merriman was in Washington, D.C. It was a friend calling to offer him a job at the new Mauna Lani Hotel on the Big Island. "It took me less than 5 minutes to decide that I wanted to live in Hawaii."

Many people come from all over to enjoy a delicious, creatively prepared and presented taste of Hawaii's Regional Cuisine at Merriman's Restaurant. Chef Peter Merriman says, "It's one of America's great regional cuisines. It combines classic French and Continental cooking techniques with the use of local fish, meat, vegetables, fruits and herbs." He has received recognition from across the country for his creative and unique use of fresh Island ingredients. He has been called, "one of the best chefs in America," by noted food and wine authority, Robert Lawrence Balzer of Travel/Holiday Magazine.

Merriman and his wife Vicki opened Merriman's Restaurant in 1988. A pleasing color scheme, fun, colorful art, classical music and potted palm trees create a wonderful ambiance which is pleasant and comfortable.

For an appetizer that features a sampling of the fresh local ingredients try the Kahua Beef, Keahole Shrimp and Shiitake Mushroom Kebobs. One of Merriman's original signature items, which is highly acclaimed, is the Original Wok Charred Ahi (recipe at right). For dessert their Coconut Brûleé is divine—so smooth, creamy and delicately flavored.

Lunch Monday through Friday, under $10.00. Dinner nightly. Entrees $12.50–$24.00. Reservations recommended.

Shrimp with Corn and Black Beans

1 Pound (16–20)	Shrimp, peeled and deveined		2 Teaspoons	Fresh Ginger, minced
			½ Teaspoon	Sugar
1 ½ Tablespoons	Vegetable Oil		1 Tablespoon	Butter
2 Ears	Fresh Corn, cut from the cob		½ Cup	Green Onion Tops, cut on the bias
1 Teaspoon	Fresh Garlic, minced		2 Tablespoons	Cilantro
1 Teaspoon	Shallots, minced		½ Teaspoons	Salt, or to Taste
¼ Cup	Chinese Salted Black Beans		2 Cups	Mixed Salad Greens
			1	Tomato, cut into wedges

Heat vegetable oil in a 10" sauté pan. Add shrimp and sear on both sides until just pink. Remove from pan. Add the corn, ginger, garlic, and shallots and sauté until corn is just cooked, about two minutes. Add the shrimp and black beans, butter, and sugar. Toss and cook one minute. Add the green onions and toss. Add salt to taste. Arrange the greens on four plates. Place the shrimp mixture on top of the greens, and garnish with cilantro and tomato wedges. An appetizer for four.

Wok Charred Ahi

½ Cup	Clarified Butter		½ Teaspoon	Cayenne Pepper
2 Teaspoons	Fresh Grated Ginger		1 Teaspoon	Salt
2 Teaspoons	Chopped Shallots		½	Lemon, juice only
2 Teaspoons	Crushed Chilies		2 pieces	8 Ounce Ahi Logs, scored on top for cutting logs, cut 4" long by 1¼" square
1 Teaspoon	Fresh Chopped Thyme			
2 Teaspoons	Crushed Garlic			
1 Teaspoon	Fresh Chopped Marjoram			

Mix together clarified butter, ginger, shallots, chilies, thyme, garlic, marjoram, cayenne pepper, salt, and lemon juice. Heat wok until metal begins turning white. Dredge Ahi logs in butter mixture, then sear in wok 20 seconds on each side. Slice and serve. Note: The sauce we use is 4 parts Shoyu (soy sauce), 1 part Mirin, 1 part lime juice and Wasabi to taste. Wasabi must be made into a thick paste with water first; ¼ cup Wasabi to 2 cups Shoyu (this is the Sashimi dip). Fresh tropical fruit makes an excellent accompaniment.

As you walk into Bamboo, you will feel that you are stepping back in time to the real "Old Hawaii". In restoring the 80-year-old Takata General Store (which began as a hotel—owned and built by the Harada Family), owners Joan and John Channon have tried to maintain the original architecture.

You will experience lots of aloha at Bamboo. Friendly Hawaiian "aunties" will entertain you as they serve you. Always surprises, there may be impromptu entertainment from any member of the staff who becomes inspired. Bamboo is not only an authentic and fascinating experience for the visitor, but a gathering place for the community as well.

They serve great fresh Hawaiian food with an Asian flair. Local farmers supply their organic produce. Their delicious Clam Chowder, made with coconut milk and ulu (bread fruit, in place of the potatoes), was written about in the Boston Globe. Try their Eggs Bamboo for Sunday Brunch, or their specialty, Chicken Saté Pot Stickers, for lunch. They have a daily vegetarian special and famous Lilikoi Margaritas!

The Gallery at Bamboo features Island made art and handicrafts.

Entertainment is offered on some evenings, including Karaoke on Friday nights. Lunch Tuesday through Saturday $5.00–$8.00. Dinner Tuesday through Saturday $7.00–$15.00. Sunday Brunch $3.00–$9.00.

It's worth the drive to Hawi! (Pronounced Hah vee).

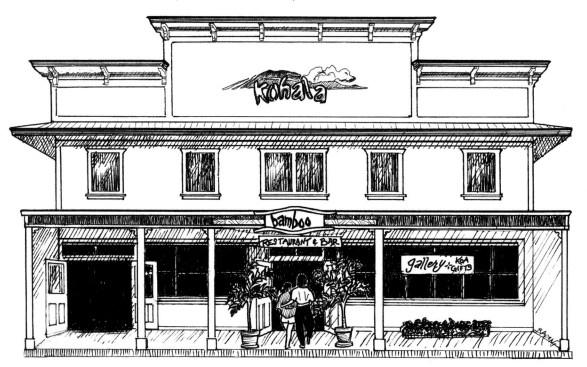

Hot Spinach Salad with Papaya Seed Dressing

Papaya Seed Dressing

2 Tablespoons	Papaya Seeds		¾ Cup	Sugar
¼ Cup	Onion, chopped		1 Tablespoon	Salt
¾ Cup	Red Wine Vinegar		¾ Cup	Canola Oil
1 Tablespoon	Dry Mustard			

Blend first 6 ingredients, using 1 tablespoon of the papaya seeds. Add other 1 tablespoon of the seeds, then slowly add oil and adjust to taste. This makes approximately 1 pint which keeps well and can be used as a marinade as well as a dressing.

Spinach Salad

2-3 Pounds	Fresh Spinach		4 Tablespoons	Crumbled Feta Cheese
½	Papaya, sliced			

Sauté the following together in the papaya seed dressing:

½	Fresh Red Pepper, julienned		½ Pound	Fresh Mushrooms, sliced
½	Red Onion, thinly sliced		¼ Cup	Pinenuts

Arrange the fresh spinach leaves on a plate, and when mushrooms are lightly cooked, arrange over the spinach and then pour hot dressing over the salad. Garnish with papaya slices and crumbled feta cheese.

Settle down into a large comfortable chair and enjoy the beautiful and elegant surroundings you will find at the highly recommended Donatoni's. You will experience superb Italian cuisine, which the chef calls "The New Authentic Italian Cuisine"—"Authentic" for the traditional flavors, "New" because it is lighter and healthier.

The interior architecture and decor is beautiful and well executed. For outdoor dining, enjoy the terrace by a peaceful lagoon with lush tropical gardens. A tantalizingly romantic place to watch the sunset.

Dining at Donatoni's, you will be in well-known company. On one wall they have interesting photographs of Tom Cruise and Nicole Kidman, Billy Crystal, Liza Minnelli, and more who have also dined here.

The chef recommends the Insalata Di Mare con Cannellini and the Zebra Ravioli Alla Vecchia Genova—black and white ravioli filled with ricotta and parmesan cheeses, served in a creamy pesto sauce. And for dessert, the Panna Cotta. Full dinners are also served at the bar where I heard you will be pampered and told stories by interesting and entertaining bartenders. Dinner only. Entrees $18.00–$29.50. Call for reservations and nights open.

Vitello Ala Sorrentina

12	2 Ounce Veal Scaloppini		2 Ounces	Olive Oil
½ Cup	Tomato Coulis			Salt and Pepper to Taste
4 Slices	Proscuitto		1½ Teaspoon	Basil Chiffonade
12 Slices	Eggplant, lightly sautéed, sliced		12 Slices	Buffalo Mozzarella

Lightly season the veal with salt and pepper. Place basil chiffonade and proscuitto slices on top of the veal. Heat a sauté pan and add olive oil. Sauté the veal on both sides until medium rare. Drain off the oil and cover the top of each scaloppini with the eggplant, then mozzarella. Brown under the broiler. Place tomato coulis on a plate, and display the veal on top of the sauce. Serves four.

Pasta Con Aragosta

1 Pound	Lobster Tail, diced			Salt and Pepper to Taste
12 Ounces	Angel Hair Pasta, cooked			Chives to Taste
1 Cup	Asparagus Stems, pureed			Olive Oil as needed
1½ Cup	Cream		1 Cup	Asparagus Tips, sliced
2 Ounces	Butter			

Heat some olive oil in a non–stick pan, and sauté the pasta. Meanwhile, in another pan, reduce together the cream, asparagus puree, butter, lobster meat and the seasoning. When almost done, add the asparagus tips in the sauce and the warm pasta. When hot, place the pasta in a plate and pour the rest of the sauce over the pasta. Serves four.

Terrina Di Melanzane

1 Sheet	Gelatin Sheet		3 Ounces	Balsamic Vinaigrette (1
1½	Eggplant, sliced ½" thick			Part Balsamic Vinegar to 3
1	Roasted Red Pepper			Parts Olive Oil, Salt &
1	Roasted Yellow Pepper			Pepper)

Garnish

2 Tablespoons	Pecorino Cheese with Truffles		½ Tablespoon	Italian Parsley
Few Drops	Olive Oil		2 Tablespoons	Tomato Coulis

Line mold with plastic wrap. In a separate bowl, add gelatin sheet into warm dressing and allow to soften. Roast and peel peppers and remove seeds. Grill eggplant. Fill mold by alternating layers of dressing and vegetables. Cover and refrigerate until firm. Garnish plate with tomato coulis, oil, Pecorino cheese and Italian parsley.

Colorful Koi fish swim in the tranquil pond that almost surrounds Imari. Water lilies float lightly on the surface. A beautiful and peaceful setting outside prepares you to enter a different world, and experience a different culture inside.

Japanese music adds to the authentic ambiance, and you will notice that Imari is very popular with visitors from Japan. Japanese cooking is a very artistic endeavor which you can experience with a choice of 3 different styles. Teppanyaki is a style where you are seated around the grill and have a close up view of the chef preparing your dinner. It is fun to watch prawns being prepared in this manner. The Sushi Bar is excellent and offers many delicious fresh choices. Shabu–Shabu is a traditional Japanese dining experience served table side and set over an open flame burner at your table. The Shabu–Shabu Beef for two is a popular choice. Other popular entrées include the Tempuras, Sukiyaki, and the Filet Mignon and Lobster Tail for two.

For a very special dinner, reserve the private individual tea house shown here.

All dinners are served with Salad, Steamed Rice, Miso Soup, Pickled Vegetables and Japanese Green Tea. $22.00–$45.00. Call for reservations and nights open.

156

Teriyaki Chicken Breast

4	8–Ounce Boneless Chicken Breasts	½ Cup	Mirin
	Salt and Pepper to Taste	½ Cup	Sake
2 Ounces	Tempura Flour	4 Ounces	Teriyaki Sauce (see recipe below)
2 Ounces	Sterling Oil	2 Tablespoons	Chopped Green Onions

Teriyaki Sauce

½ Cup	Soy Sauce	3 Tablespoons	Sake
¾ Cup	Mirin	4 Teaspoons	Tamari Sauce

Season chicken breast with salt and pepper, dredge in flour. Heat oil, brown chicken, and deglaze with Mirin and Sake. Simmer until chicken is done.

In a separate pan, mix together ingredients for teriyaki sauce and bring to a simmer. Place chicken on a plate and sauce with Teriyaki Sauce. Sprinkle with green onions. Serve with steamed rice. Serves four.

Asari Butter Clams

4 Dozen	Clams	3 Tablespoons	Green Onions, chopped
1½ Cups	Dashi	½ Cup	Butter
2 Ounces	Shoyu		

Place clams with Dashi and Shoyu in a sauté pan and steam clams open. Add all of the butter and whisk in broth. Sprinkle with green onions before serving.

BACON

Enjoying an excursion to the Kamuela Provision Company allows you to experience all the magnificent wonder of the gorgeous grounds at the Hilton. Starting from the lobby you can ride a boat or tram to get to the restaurant. Or, it's fun to walk and explore, go over bridges and see the dolphin pond. Many natural looking pools, tropical gardens and waterfalls create an incredible ambiance which you can continue to enjoy while dining at Kamuela Provision Company.

The interior is rich and elegant, yet casual. Dining on the lanai provides a spectacular sunset view with waves breaking nearby, while a live solo guitarist plays contemporary Hawaiian music.

They serve great fresh fish there. Most of the servers surf and fish during the day and bring a lot of knowledge about fish and the ocean to you in the evenings. So feel free to ask questions. Don't miss the Humuhumunukunukuapuaa (Hawaii's State Fish) in the large aquarium to the left as you walk into the restaurant.

Check out the Kamuela Provision Company store for a variety of locally made items you can take home with you.

Dinner only. $18.00–$29.00. Call for reservations and nights open.

Fire Cracker Scallops

20	Large Scallops		Salt and Pepper to Taste
4	1" Thick Pineapple Slices with skin on	⅓ Teaspoon	Red Curry Paste
		⅓ Teaspoon	Lemon Grass, finely chopped
8 Tablespoons	Roasted Red Pepper Aioli		
2	Lemons	½ Teaspoon	Garlic, minced
1 Teaspoon	Butter	½ Teaspoon	Ginger, minced

First prepare the Aioli (recipe below).

Season scallops with salt and pepper, red curry paste, lemon grass, garlic and ginger. Sauté in hot butter. When cooked, place on pineapple slice and drizzle with Roasted Red Pepper Aioli; garnish with lemon. Serves four.

Roasted Red Pepper Aioli

1	Red Bell Pepper	1½ Ounces	White Wine
2 Tablespoons	Onions	1½ Ounces	Chicken Stock
½ Teaspoon	Chopped Garlic		Salt and Pepper to Taste
½ Teaspoon	Chopped Shallots	6 Ounces	Mayonnaise

Roast, seed and peel pepper. Return to large saucepan. Combine garlic, onions, shallots, (all finely chopped) white wine and chicken stock. Reduce until all liquid is gone, Blend until puree is smooth. Cool, then add mayonnaise and mix well. Put aside.

For Charred Ahi with Three Bean Rice from Kamuela Provision Company, see page 191.

A charming and intimate atmosphere will greet you as you walk into Bangkok Houses. This fabulous Thai restaurant is owned by a family from Thailand with 10 years of experience in owning and operating Thai restaurants.

Bangkok Houses offers an incredible menu with over 100 choices on the dinner menu and many for lunch. They will also prepare special requests to accommodate customers. Some of the herbs they use—lemon grass, Thai basil, and mint, are grown in their own garden at home. Many of their entrées are available with a choice of chicken, beef, pork, shrimp or squid. And there are many vegetarian choices. Their steamed dumplings are unique and tasty (stuffed with shrimp, chicken, bamboo shoots, mushrooms and water chestnuts). Popular items include their Papaya Salad, and their Sizzling Chicken or Seafood. The Pineapple Fried Rice includes a combination of shrimp, chicken, cashew nuts and raisins baked in a pineapple shell just before serving. Yumm.

When I asked what they do to make their customers happy, I was met with a smile and this answer: "Homemade lychee ice cream, fried ice cream, fried banana." So be sure to try one.

They also offer catering and takeout. Lunch Monday–Friday, $4.00–$8.00. Dinner nightly $5.00–$19.00.

Chicken Satay

2 Pounds	Chicken Breasts, cut in 1" strips		1 Teaspoon	Salt
3 Slices	Crushed Ginger		2 Tablespoons	Butter
3 Cloves	Crushed Garlic		3 Tablespoons	Light Cream
1 Tablespoon	Curry Powder		½ Cup	Coconut Milk
1 Tablespoon	Coriander Powder			Satay Sticks

Knead chicken with the other ingredients, adding one ingredient at a time. Marinate for at least 2 hours. Thread a few pieces of chicken on the top half of each satay stick. Cook over charcoal. While cooking, sprinkle coconut milk on the chicken.

Sauce

1 Tablespoon	Red Curry Paste		1½ Cups	Coconut Milk or Cream
1 Tablespoon	Roasted Chili Curry Paste		1 Tablespoon	Lemon Juice or Tamarind Juice
1 Tablespoon	Sugar			
2 Tablespoons	Peanut Butter		1 Teaspoon	Salt

Heat the coconut milk until boiling. Add the 2 kinds of curry paste and stir fry. Add peanut butter, sugar, salt and tamarind juice or lemon juice. The sauce should have a salty, sweet and slightly sour taste. Chicken Satay makes an excellent hors d'oeuvre. Serve with cucumber salad.

Tom Kha Gai—Coconut Soup

½ Pound	Chicken Chunks		3 Medium	Hot Peppers Diced
½ Can	Coconut Milk		2 Teaspoons	Fresh Fish Sauce
2 Cans	Chicken Broth		6 Teaspoons	Lime Sauce
1 Sprig	Chopped Lemon Grass		½ Cup	Mushrooms
3 Slices	Galanga Root			Cilantro for Garnish

Boil chicken in broth until tender, add ingredients in order listed. Yield: four servings.

"I can't believe I just discovered your restaurant when it's my last night here." Those are words that owners Peter and Ann Weinstock hear too often about their wonderful Sibu Cafe. When people discover this little gem they like going back again to enjoy the exciting Indonesian cuisine that is served there. As Peter says, "I don't serve boring food."

What they do serve is generous portions of fresh, tasty food (no MSG) with exotic flavors. Their Balinese Chicken is very popular—boneless chicken marinated in tarragon, garlic and onions, cooked over the open flame, and covered with peanut sauce. The combination plates are huge and allow you to taste a delicious selection of Stirfry, Curry and Saté. Try their Nasi Udek (fragrant rice made with coconut milk, lemon grass,

Kaffir lime leaves and turmeric) with your entrée. They offer many choices for vegetarians.

The courtyard atmosphere is relaxed and casual. Unusual Indonesian art adorns the walls, including lots of masks. Fabric from antique sarongs from Bali and Java, is set under glass on some of the tables.

Most of the staff has been with Sibu Cafe a long time because they enjoy the many compliments they receive from customers about the food.

Sibu Cafe is tucked in the Banyan Court Mall, across from the sea wall (where the waves sometimes splash over onto the road). Turn on Lakani Street (one—way) to park behind Sibu Cafe. Lunch $7.00–$11.00. Dinner $9.00–$13.00. Open daily.

Pais Udang or Shrimp Packages

2 Pounds	Large Shrimp or Prawns		1	Medium Lime
6	Macadamia Nuts		1	Fresh Sprig of Basil or Mint
1 Ounce	Ginger Root			
½ Teaspoon	Turmeric		1	Bay Leaf
3	Jalapeños (or other hot chilies)			Salt
6	Green Onions or Scallions		1	Banana Leaf (or aluminum foil)

Clean, wash and drain the shrimp, put in a bowl, sprinkle lightly with salt, and set aside. In a food processor (or mortar and pestle), place the mac nuts, ginger and turmeric and grind them together until fine. Seed the chilies and slice them finely. Slice the lime into thin rounds, discarding the seeds. Chop the green onion into ½ inch pieces. Mix all these ingredients together with the shrimp, add a little more salt and that's the filling. Place some of the mixture on a piece of banana leaf (or aluminum foil), lay the herbs on top and fold into an oblong package. Toothpicks work nicely to hold the package closed. Steam or bake (at 350 degrees) for 15 minutes then transfer the package to a hot skillet and cook it for 5 to 10 minutes in order to reduce some of the liquid. Serves 4 to 6.

Fried Tofu with Spicy Lime Sauce

	Tofu cut into ½ or ⅝ inch squares		½ Cup	Water
2 Cloves	Garlic		2 Tablespoons	Fish Sauce
1½	Hot Red Seeded Chilies		½ Cup	Fresh Lime Juice
			3 Tablespoons	Brown Sugar

For the dipping sauce, combine the garlic, chilies and water in blender or food processor until the ingredients are minced. Combine the fish sauce, lime juice and sugar in a bowl. Add the contents from the food processor. Deep fry the tofu in a wok or deep pan until the cubes are slightly puffy and a little browned. Stick each cube with a toothpick and just dip away.

(Peter says, "I have seen this dish, single-handedly cause tofu-haters to change their minds about this increasingly popular source of protein.")

The wonderful aroma of fresh baking bread and cinnamon rolls will lure you into Island Lava Java in the morning. In the evening you will be drawn in by live Hawaiian music with hula dancing, classical guitar, or other live entertainment. Any time of day it's a great place to relax, enjoy the ocean view, and watch people go by.

Relish a cup of freshly brewed espresso, or a refreshing fresh fruit sorbet (try the mango or the coconut, mmm). Lava Java Road is their custom ice cream flavor freshly made especially for them by Tropical Dreams, right on the Big Island. They also serve a Lava Java cake and many choices of both local (Kona) and International coffees.

Lava Java also offers sandwiches, fresh homemade soup (usually vegetarian), and many unique and delicious baked goods. This is a casual, serve-yourself type of place—if you can decide what to choose from—a variety of filled scones, outrageous muffins, macadamia nut cookies, and more. Everything is so delicious!

People enjoy coming here to watch the sunset over the ocean while sipping a cappuccino. What a fabulous place to enjoy an evening with live entertainment (7 nights a week) and a first class sunset ocean view, for only $5.00–$10.00. Open daily, 7:00 a.m. through 10:00 p.m.

Lava Java Cake with Cappuccino Butter Cream Icing

4 Ounces	Unsweetened Chocolate		2⅓ Cups	Flour
½ Cup	Water		2 Teaspoons	Baking Powder
3	Eggs		¾ Teaspoon	Baking Soda
½ Pound	Soft Butter		Dash	Salt
2 Cups	Dark Brown Sugar		1 Cup	Sour Cream

Preheat oven to 350 degrees. Combine chocolate and water, microwave in 20 second intervals until chocolate has just melted. Set aside and cool. Once cooled, whisk in beaten eggs. In mixer, beat butter and sugar until light and fluffy, then add chocolate mixture and beat until smooth. In separate bowl, combine flour, baking powder, soda, and salt. With mixer on low speed, add half of the dry ingredients to the chocolate mixture followed by the sour cream, and then the rest of the dry ingredients. Pour batter evenly into three round cake pans that have been greased and floured. Bake for 45 minutes or until knife inserted in the middle comes out clean.

Icing

1 Cup	White Sugar		½ Pound	Soft Butter
⅓ Cup	Water		1 Shot	Espresso
6	Egg Yolks		2 Tablespoons	Instant Coffee

Combine sugar and water in a saucepan and bring to a boil without stirring until mixture has reached 250 degrees (approximately 8–10 minutes). Beat egg yolks in a mixer until thick, then slowly pour sugar mixture into eggs and mix for 10 minutes. Slowly add butter, one tablespoon at a time and mix. Pour in espresso mixed with the instant coffee. Refrigerate until icing thickens. Generously frost cake and enjoy with a hot cup of Lava Java coffee!

Lava Java's Basic Scones

1½ Cups	Flour		½ Pound	Firm Butter, cut into pieces
1½ Cups	Cake Flour			
¼ Cup	Sugar		1	Egg
1 Tablespoon	Baking Powder		½ Tablespoon	Water
¾ Teaspoon	Salt		¾ Cup	Heavy Cream

Preheat oven to 350 degrees. Combine the first five ingredients in a mixer bowl and stir to combine. Cut butter pieces into flour mixture as you would a biscuit recipe. In a small bowl whisk together egg, water and cream. Add to flour until combined. Do not over mix! Turn out dough onto a lightly floured surface, and knead*, adding flour until dough is still quite soft yet manageable. It is very important not to overwork the dough. Roll out dough ½" thick and use a cookie/biscuit cutter to cut out scones. Brush tops with egg white and sprinkle with sugar. Bake 20 minutes.

*(During kneading phase, cheddar cheese and chives, cinnamon and raisins, blueberries or other items may be added.)

The food at Thai Rin Restaurant is exotic and outstanding. It is truly authentic Thai cuisine based on the cuisine of Bangkok and Central Thailand. The family that owns and operates Thai Rin brought their chef over from Thailand after their first year in business on the Big Island.

For a delicious appetizer, try their Chicken Satay—world famous strips of chicken on bamboo skewers served with peanut dipping sauce and cucumber salad. (It was really good!) One of their most popular specialties is the Pad Thai Fried Noodles Thai Style—soft Thai noodles with fresh shrimp and golden egg. (Recipe on next page.) Or try one of their flavorful Curries—red, green, yellow, or Panang (peanut curry), with choice of chicken, beef or pork. They also offer many delicious seafood specialties and an assortment of vegetarian entrées, which are listed on their dinner menu but are available at lunch also—just ask.

I enjoyed my first experience with a creamy Thai iced tea—refreshing, delicious, and unique. Try one. Thai Rin is located across from the ocean and is the place to enjoy sunset dining with exotic food! Lunch served Monday through Saturday. $7.00–$11.00. Dinner nightly $8.00–$16.00.

Pad Thai (Fried Noodles Thai Style)

½ Pound	Rice Noodles		1 Tablespoon	Vegetable Oil
2 Tablespoons	Thai Fish Sauce		½ Cup	Red Cabbage
2 Tablespoons	Sugar		½ Cup	Bean Sprouts
1 Tablespoon	Vinegar		1	Chopped Green Onion and
1 Tablespoon	Tamarind Sauce			Chinese Parsley
2	Eggs			Thai Condiments: Ground
6—8	Shrimps (M)			Peanut, Ground Chili
10—12 Pieces	Sliced Chicken (1/4 Pound)			Pepper, Slice of Lime, Fresh Bean Sprouts.

Soak noodles in cold water until soft. Heat oil in wok. Stir fry chicken, shrimp, and eggs. Add fish sauce, vinegar, tamarind, and sugar. Add noodles, cabbage and bean sprouts to mixture and continue stir frying. Put mixture on plate. Garnish with fresh beans sprouts, green onion, Chinese parsley, and lime. Serve with Thai condiments. Serves 2–4.

Panang Curry (With Beef or Chicken)

1 Tablespoon	Panang Curry Paste		½ Pound	Sliced Beef or Chicken
1 Can	Coconut Milk (19 Ounce)		½ Cup	Sliced Green Bean and
2 Tablespoons	Thai Fish Sauce			Bamboo Shoots
1 Tablespoon	Sugar		6–7	Basil Leaves

Heat ¼ can of coconut milk in pan or pot. Add curry paste and stir. Add meat, fish sauce, and sugar to mixture and continue stir frying until the meat is cooked. Add vegetables and the rest of the coconut milk. Place the mixture on a plate or bowl. Garnish with sweet basil. Serves two.

At the highly recommended Palm Cafe an incredible dining experience awaits you. It is owned by Chef Daniel Thiebaut and Brian Anderson. While Chef Daniel is known for his masterful and creative culinary expertise, he explains how everyone at Palm Cafe plays an integral part in creating a wonderful feeling and dining experience for their guests. The chairs are intentionally comfortable in the beautiful and elegant, yet casual setting. A view of Kailua Bay and the open air atmosphere adds to the ambiance.

Growing up in France, Chef Daniel began his apprenticeship at age thirteen, after which he lived and worked in Switzerland, Jamaica, England, the Philippines, and other places. In Hawaii, the personal connection he has developed with the farmers inspires him to use fresh grown food creatively, beautifully and tastefully. The presentation is exquisite, the food is outstanding.

The cuisine is Pacific Rim with a blend of Asian and French influences. They offer a variety of unique fresh Hawaiian fish with outstanding flavors and textures as well as fabulous meat, foul, and vegetarian selections. Signature items include: Chinese Stuffed Ravioli, Hawaiian Snapper with Crushed Mustard Seed and Szechwan Peppercorns, and for dessert, Chocolate Croquant. They feature an exceptional wine list and free tasting.

Dinner nightly. Entrees $14.50–$23.00. Reservations recommended.

Chinese Stuffed Ravioli

Pasta

4 Teaspoons	Warm Water		2	Egg Whites
2 Cups	Flour		½ Teaspoon	Salt
2	Eggs		2 Tablespoons	Peanut Oil

Place all ingredients except water in food processor bowl. Pulse several times. Add water and pulse until dough forms being sure NOT to overmix. Cover with foil and let rest for 30 minutes.

Filling

1 Pound	Bok Choy Leaves, chopped		2 Tablespoons	Chinese Parsley, chopped fine
1 Tablespoon	Olive Oil			
1 Pound	Ground Pork		½ Teaspoon	Chili Garlic Sauce
½ Teaspoon	Ground Pepper		1	Egg

Heat oil in skillet over medium heat. Add ground pork and brown. Drain excess fat, add bok choy leaves, and cook for one minute. Transfer pork and bok choy to bowl and cool. Blend together in food processor. Add salt and pepper to taste. Add parsley and chili garlic sauce. Place filling in center of cut ravioli, seal with a mixture the egg and one tablespoon of water, and form ravioli to desired size. Boil in salted water for two minutes.

Sauce

2 Tablespoons	Balsamic Vinegar		2 Tablespoons	Butter
1 Teaspoon	Ginger		1 Tablespoon	Chives
1 Cup	Sherry Wine			Salt and Pepper to Taste
1 Cup	Cream			

Make sauce in the same way as a basic beurre blanc. Pour over ravioli and serve.

For Chocolate Croquant with Ginger–Vanilla Bean Sauce from Palm Cafe, see page 192.

The Burgundy region of France is known for superb food and wine, as is La Bourgogne (pronounced Bor–goan–yuh) which means Burgundy. With owners Ron Gallaher and Colleen Moore offering their warm and personal attention to each guest in their restaurant, you are assured a very special dining experience.

Ron is also the chef, and creates "the simple, flavorful food of the Burgundy region of France" from very fresh local ingredients. Colleen was named #1 Waitress in West Hawaii Today's Survey. La Bourgogne was rated #2 for the "Best Place to Dine" in Kona.

They have created a delightful bit of France in their small, intimate and charming restaurant. Each month they feature a unique price fix menu offering a full meal, from salad through dessert, with 2 types of wine to complement your dinner. This is usually $40.00 per person and is a wonderful way to pamper yourself.

Popular items on their regular menu include Poisson du jour, their fresh catch of the day ("which features only the best fish caught each day from local waters"). Another favorite is Supreme de Canard, sauce bigarde–sliced breast of roast duck with lemon/orange sauce. They have fabulous desserts including their decadent Chocolate Mousse, Amaretto Cheesecake, and a special dessert daily. A variety of quality wines are offered from Burgundy and California. Dinner entrées $16.00–$28.00. Reservations recommended. Open Monday through Saturday.

Veal Shanks with Baby Vegetables

2¾ Pounds	Veal Shank/Osso Bucco	½ Pound	Baby Carrots, peeled and cut in half lengthwise
4 Tablespoons	Butter		Large Carrots, pared or quartered
1 Clove	Garlic Whole and unpeeled for the meat	1 Pound	New Potatoes peeled and cut in half lengthwise
3	Tomatoes	1 Clove	Garlic, whole and unpeeled for vegetables
½ Cup	Red Wine, Burgundy		
2 Tablespoons	Butter for the Vegetables		
1 Tablespoon	Olive Oil		

Salt and pepper the shank before cooking over moderate heat. Melt 4 tablespoons butter in a pot just large enough to hold the veal. When hot, add the veal and a clove of garlic, and brown for 15 minutes turning frequently. Add the tomatoes and wine, cover the pot and lower the heat and simmer for 1½ hours, turning the meat occasionally. While the meat finishes cooking, heat 2 tablespoons butter and 1 tablespoon oil. Add the carrots and potatoes, garlic, salt and pepper. Cook the vegetables until lightly browned, then lower the heat and cook very slowly for 15 to 20 minutes or until done, shaking the pan frequently. To serve, lift the meat out of the pot and season with salt and pepper. Place on a hot platter, surround with the vegetables. Taste the cooking liquid for salt and pepper. Adjust if needed and serve in a sauce boat on the side.

Roasted Red Pepper Soup

2½ Pounds	Whole Red Bell Peppers, roasted, peeled, and seeded, or a 28 ounce can of Roasted Red Peppers	½ Teaspoon	Cayenne
		6 Ounces	Tomato Juice
		2 Ounces	Tomato Paste
		2 Ounces	Lemon Juice
2	Medium Yellow Onions diced	2 Ounces	Olive Oil
		8 Cups	Chicken Stock or Water
1 Tablespoon	Chopped Garlic	1 Cup	Whipping Cream

In a thick bottomed pot, sauté the onions and garlic in the olive oil over medium heat until the onions are clear. Add roasted peppers, tomato products, cayenne and lemon juice. Stir well and add half of stock/water. Bring soup to a simmer. Add the rest of the stock/water and bring to a simmer. Let cook 30 to 40 minutes. Puree the whole soup in a food processor or blender. Return to pot and adjust seasoning to taste using salt and white pepper. Finish with the whipping cream. Be careful not to bring cream to a boil. Garnish with a sprig of flat leaf parsley. Yield: 8 servings.

Sitting on the terrace at Edward's, I felt incredibly relaxed with the ocean breeze blowing gently across my face, the waves breaking just below, and soft jazz floating through the air. The ambiance is alluring and magical, a great place for romance.

Edward's at the Terrace features outstanding exotic Mediterranean cuisine in a beautiful, covered outdoor dining area. The music changes from old Hawaiian, to female vocalists, to instrumental jazz classics and blues.

Edward Frady, chef and owner, started cooking as a hobby in 1979. He then trained in France and New York, and now teaches in the University of Hawaii–West Hawaii Culinary Arts Program. He is also President of the Chef de Cuisine Association.

Enjoy a banana macadamia nut waffle and homemade apple spice sausage patty for breakfast. For lunch a popular entrée is Tanginine Chicken stuffed in papaya. Edward's daily specials are seasonal and include exotic items such as Ragout of Mushrooms in a pomegranate sauce, served with puff pastry and fresh basil, for an appetizer. For dinner– Peppered Broadbill–grilled, pepper crusted and served with Mediterranean olives and garlic Beurre–Blanc sauce.

Open Tuesday through Sunday. Breakfast $5.50–$9.00. Lunch $7.50–$11.00. Dinner entrées $15.00–$29.00.

Edward's is a little tricky to find, but well worth the effort. From Highway 11 or Alii Drive turn towards the ocean on Kamehameha III, turn right on Manukai Street. Follow to the end and then ask at the information booth at Kanaloa Condominiums. Walk into the pool area and go right.

Mushroom Pomegranate Ragout

1 Tablespoon	Olive Oil		1 Splash	Brandy
1 Small	Shallot, sliced		¼ Cup	White Wine
1 Cup	Mushrooms		¼ Cup	Cream
¼ Cup	Dried Mushrooms		1 Drop	Worcestershire Sauce
½ Teaspoon	Herbs de Provence		1 Ounce	Mushroom Juice
1 Teaspoon	Garlic, crushed		4 Pieces	Whole Basil Leaves
2 Teaspoons	Pomegranate Juice		1 Piece	Puff Pastry Shell

Sauté shallots until soft, add garlic, sauté but do not brown. Add brandy, wine and pomegranate juice. Simmer to reduce by one–half. Add mushrooms, mushroom juice, Worcestershire Sauce, herbs, and cream. Season with salt and pepper. Use as a filling for puff pastry. Garnish with whole basil leaves. Serves one.

Chicken/Duck Liver Mousseline

8 Ounces	Chicken/Duck Livers		2 Ounces	Butter, cut into 8 pieces
3 Tablespoons	Butter		2 Ounces	Heavy Cream
3 Tablespoons	Minced Shallots		1 Tablespoon	Tawny Port
2 Ounces	Tawny Port			Salt and Pepper to Taste

Sauté chicken livers, (which have been patted dry) in 3 tablespoons of butter over moderate heat. Turn them for 4 minutes or until browned on the outside but still pink within. Transfer the livers with a slotted spoon to the food processor with the chopping blade in place.

Add minced shallots to the skillet and cook over moderate heat, stirring for 3 minutes until softened. Add 2 ounces Tawny Port to deglaze the skillet, scraping up the brown bits clinging to the bottom and sides. Reduce the liquid over high heat to about 1 tablespoon. Transfer the liquid to the food processor bowl and process with the livers. Force the mixture through a food mill and into a bowl. Allow to cool, covered with a buttered round of wax paper.

Return the puree to the food processor and with the motor running, add the rest of the butter, one piece at a time, being sure to incorporate each piece before adding the next and blend until the mixture is smooth.

Transfer the mixture to a bowl, fold in the heavy cream and 1 tablespoon of tawny port with a rubber spatula. Add salt and pepper to taste. Chill the Mousseline, covered for at least an hour or until firm, but of spreading consistency. Yield: 6 servings.

It is such a treat to eat at Aloha Cafe. You will want to try it early in your visit so you can go back again. They have so many delicious choices for every meal and in between!

Aloha Cafe is located in the historic Aloha Theatre in Kainaliu, built in 1932. The theatre shows a variety of great plays on most weekends. (A hilarious female version of the Odd Couple was playing when I was there.)

Aloha Cafe features delicious homemade breads and pastries, fresh squeezed juices, fresh muffins and hearty breakfasts. Lunch features great burgers, delicious homemade soups, vegetarian specials, Mexican food and always the "freshest Island fish".

The Aloha chefs create interesting and tasteful specials at every meal. Sit on the lanai and sip a pure Kona Coffee or espresso and enjoy one of their incredible desserts—Rhubarb Linzertorte, or a Blueberry Lemon Torte topped with real whipped cream (so good it melts in your mouth!) and many more.

Aloha Cafe has been featured in Food and Wine, Bon Appétit, and Gourmet Magazine. Hidden Hawaii and Frommer's gave Aloha Cafe top ratings.

The atmosphere is friendly and casual. It's located south of Kona on Highway 11 before you get to Kealakekua.

Open 8 to 8 daily and Sunday Brunch 9 to 2.

Breakfast and Lunch $2.50–$8.00.

Dinner $7.00–$16.00.

174

Papaya Seed Dressing

1 Cup	White Wine Vinegar	1½ Teaspoons	Salt
¼ Cup + 2 Tbs	Lemon Juice	5 Cloves	Garlic
¾ Cup	Honey	1 Teaspoon	Pepper
½ Cup	Fresh Parsley	3 Cups	Soybean Oil
1 Teaspoon	Paprika	3	Whole, skinned papayas

Put all ingredients in a blender with oil on top. Blend well. Add 2 cups of water. Blend.

Tropical Fruit Muffins

1½ Cups	Unbleached Flour	½ Cup	Sesame Seeds
1½ Cups	Baker's Bran	1 Tablespoon	Baking Powder
1 Cup	Grated Coconut	1 Teaspoon	Baking Soda

Mix the above ingredients together.

2	Eggs	2 Cups	Milk
1 Cup	Honey	1 Cup	Mashed Bananas
½ Cup	Melted Butter	1 Cup	Crushed Pineapple

Mix in a separate bowl and stir into dry ingredients.

**(Optional) Dried Fruit,
Dates, Papayas or Mangos**

Add optional dried fruits. Bake in a muffin pan at 375 degrees for 30 minutes.

I wish I could portray to you the warmth and hospitality I felt as I sat and talked with Mary Teshima and her daughter Fumi. Mary explained how she had started Teshima's during WWII. She made friends with the soldiers, cooked for them, and they taught her how to cook hamburgers and other American food. The soldiers had a hard time pronouncing Mary's real name, Shizuko, so they called her Mary and it stuck.

Teshima's Restaurant has been in operation for over 50 years. It is truly a family restaurant, with many family members working there. Before she opened Teshima's, Mary owned an ice cream fountain and general merchandise store which she started in 1929. Mary is now in her eighties and she shares her philosophy that has brought her so much success: "Treat people special, help them feel comfortable. Serve food that everyone can enjoy from the oldest to the youngest." She calls it "country style home cooking". And it is good. All kinds of people gather here. In fact I heard that this is the place where chefs come to enjoy a meal out.

Teshima's is known for their delicious tempuras—light and fluffy. Their menu has, like Mary says, something for everyone from traditional American food to wonderful Japanese items. The atmosphere is very casual.

Breakfast, lunch and dinner served daily. $2.75–$11.00.

Note: The chefs at Teshima's Restaurant learn from each other and do not use written recipes. I feel their restaurant is so special and significant that I decided to include them in the book anyway. (They have been there over 50 years!)

More Recipes

From

Sauce for Clams, Scampi and Pasta

½ Cup	Clarified Butter	1 Cup	Milk or Half and Half
½ Cup	Flour	½ Cup	Garlic Butter
½ Cup	Chablis	1⅛ Teaspoon	Lemon Juice
1 Cup	Chicken Stock	1⅛ Teaspoon	Caper Juice

Cover bottom of sauté pan with clarified butter, slowly add enough flour to absorb all butter. Cook flour well but do not brown. Add Chablis and slowly stir in chicken stock, slowly add milk, caper juice and lemon juice, and a generous helping of garlic butter. Simmer slowly but do not boil.

For scampi, add clarified butter into a saucepan with Chablis, add floured shrimp into roux. Add flour gradually into roux with chicken stock and milk. Cook over medium heat, do not burn.

For Poipu Pasta, add chopped veggies into sauce and cook vegetables until slightly crisp and pour over pasta.

For clams, clean and wash clams before adding into sauce and simmer until shells open.

For Sea Bass, same recipe as scampi. If there is no Seabass in your area, Grouper Bass, or frozen New Zealand Bass will work all the same.

Involtini d' Ono Alla Siciliana

16	3 Ounce pieces of Ono	3 Tablespoons	Olive Oil
1 Tablespoon	Ripieno Stuffing (1 table-spoon for each Ono)	1 Cup	White Wine
			Salt and Pepper to Taste

Pound the Ono gently to flatten the fish. Then spread Sicilian Stuffing on the fish and roll. Bake with olive oil and white wine at 350 degrees for 6–8 minutes. Place on top of orange tomato basil sauce (Salsa di Pomodoro Arancia e Basilico, recipe below) and serve.

Salsa di Pomodoro Arancia e Basilico (Orange Tomato Basil Sauce)

2½ Pounds	Fresh Plum Tomatoes (skinned)	3	Oranges
6	Garlic Cloves		Salt and Pepper to Taste
14	Basil Leaves	3 Tablespoons	Olive Oil

Heat olive oil in a pot. Sauté garlic and basil leaves for a few minutes, then add plum tomatoes. Lower the heat, squeez juice from halved oranges into the pot, then add the oranges. Let cook for 20 minutes. Take out oranges, and puree salsa. Add salt and pepper to taste. Serve with Ono.

Ripieno Alla Siciliana (Sicilian Stuffing for Ono)

1½ Cups	Golden Raisins	1½ Cups	Pinenuts (roasted)
12	Dry Figs	12	Anchovies
1½ Cups	Fresh Basil	¼ Cup	Italian Parsley

Soak raisins in water for 15 minutes. Put remaining ingredients and raisins in a food processor and grind until you have made a paste. Then spread on Ono and roll into to a bundle.

Poached Pears on Puff Pastry with Cinnamon Cream Anglaise and Warm Port Sauce

4	Pears, cored, cut in half lengthwise, leave stem attached		**Frozen Puff Pastry Sheet**	

Poaching Liquid

1 Cup	Port or Cabernet Wine		2	Cinnamon Sticks
½ Cup	Water		1 Cup	Raisins
½ Cup	Sugar		½ Teaspoon	Vanilla Extract
	Juice from ¼ Lemon		½ Cup	Cornstarch

Combine all ingredients (except cornstarch) in medium sauce pan, bring to slow simmer. Place halved and cored pears in liquid, let simmer 6 to 10 minutes. Remove pears and save liquid, let pears cool off. Put on plate, cover with plastic wrap and put in the refrigerator. Bring poaching liquid to full simmer. Combine cornstarch and ¼ cup cold water in a cup, mix until smooth. Add a little at a time of cornstarch mix to poaching liquid whisking steady until it starts to thicken. Keep warm or reheat later.

Cinnamon Cream Anglaise

6	Egg Yolks		2 Teaspoons	Powdered Cinnamon
4 Tablespoons	Sugar		1 Pinch	Nutmeg
1 Quart	Heavy Cream		1 Teaspoon	Vanilla

Mix cinnamon and nutmeg with sugar, add to yolks in stainless steel bowl, being held over a pot of simmering water. Add vanilla extract to yolks then whisk until sugar dissolves. Scald the heavy cream. While whisking, add the heavy cream to the sugar and mix a little at first then let rest. Whisk until it starts to thicken, making sure it does not scorch. Take it off the heat and let cool.

Defrost pastry sheet for 2 to 3 minutes. Cut the same size "v's" across a 5" strip of pastry, egg wash and place on parchment paper on a sheet pan. Bake in preheated 400 degree oven for 5 to 7 minutes. Place puff pastry triangle in the middle of a plate, take pear half and make 3 to 4 slices 1" from the top all the way to the bottom, fan out the pear and place on pastry. Pour ¼ cup of Cream Anglaise around pastry on plate. Then spoon Port Sauce over pear, let run into cream anglaise.

Garnish

1 Cup	Heavy Cream, whipped with		8 Sprigs	Mint
1 Tablespoon	Sugar			

Put in a pastry piping bag with small star tip and pipe a rosette of whipped cream at the top of the pear. Garnish with a sprig of mint next to the rosette on the pear.

Smoked Salmon and Potato Cakes with Dill Cream
—Chef Hydee Head

Dill Cream

½ Cup	Low Fat Plain Yogurt	3 Tablespoons	Chopped Fresh Dill
1 Clove	Garlic, chopped fine	½ Cup	Sour Cream
⅛ Teaspoon	Cayenne		

Stir in bowl all together, cover and chill.

Salmon Cakes

3	Large Idaho Potatoes, peeled, cut into coarse chunks	1 Tablespoon	Fresh Lemon Juice
		1 Tablespoon	Low Fat Plain Yogurt
1 Teaspoon	Olive Oil plus 3 teaspoons for frying patties	Few Drops	Tabasco
		2	Large Eggs plus 2 egg whites
6	Scallions, sliced very thin	⅛ Teaspoon	Cayenne
10 Ounces	Smoked Salmon, minced	¾ Teaspoon	Salt
½ Cup	Chopped Fresh Dill	2 Teaspoons	Unsalted Butter

Cook potatoes in boiling, salted water about 15–20 minutes, until very tender. Drain, return to pan, place on low heat to fry, about one minute. Put potatoes through a food mill, ricer, or transfer to bowl and mash. Cover. Chill at least 1 hour or overnight. Heat 1 teaspoon olive oil in non–stick skillet. Sauté scallion. Set aside. Beat eggs and whites together until smooth, add potatoes, scallions, salmon, dill, lemon juice, yogurt, cayenne, Tabasco. Mix lightly. Chill if not using right away. Just before serving, heat 1/2 teaspoon of butter and 1/2 teaspoon olive oil in non–stick skillet over medium–high heat. Gently form potato mixture into 12 patties, 2 inches wide, 1/2 inch thick (or 24 patties for hors d'oeuvres). Place 4 patties in pan, lower heat to medium and cook, shaking pan to prevent sticking, about 4 to 5 minutes. Gently flip until golden brown 3 to 4 minutes. Repeat twice. Keep patties warm in oven at 200 degrees. Serve hot with dab of dill cream and fresh sprig of dill or parsley. Serves six or 12 hors d'oeuvres.

Peanut Chicken Breast with Curry Sauce

8	Chicken Breasts (boneless, skinless halves)	3	Whole Eggs (beaten)
1 Cup	Panko	2 Tablespoons	Flour
½ Cup	Shredded Coconut (Toasted)	1 Tablespoon	Butter
1 Cup	Peanuts (dry roasted, finely chopped)	3 Tablespoons	Oil

Marinade

½ Cup	Water	½ Teaspoon	Fresh Minced Garlic
½ Cup	Shoyu	½ Teaspoon	Brown Sugar
½ Teaspoon	Fresh Minced Ginger		Orange Zest (optional)

Trim chicken; combine marinade ingredients, mix well. Add chicken; marinate at least 1 hour. Combine Panko, coconut and peanuts. Remove chicken from marinade. Dredge chicken in flour and dip in eggs, coat with Panko mixture. In a sauté pan heat butter and oil; sauté chicken over medium heat, turning once. Cook until golden brown—about 6–7 minutes. Finish in oven. Serves four.

Curry Sauce

1 Tablespoon	Peanut Oil	4 Cups	Chicken Stock
¼ Cup	Chopped Onion	1 Cup	Whipping Cream
2 Tablespoons	Chopped Celery	½ Cup	Coconut Milk
3 Tablespoons	Chopped Carrot	½ Cup	Chopped Banana (peeled)
1 Tablespoon	Curry Paste	½ Cup	Chopped Papaya (peeled and seeded)
1 Teaspoon	Whole Black Peppercorn	½ Cup	Orange Juice
1	Bay Leaf		

Heat oil in heavy saucepan over medium heat; add onion, celery, carrot, bay leaf and peppercorns. Sauté until golden brown and tender, about 5–6 minutes. Stir in curry paste, cook 2 minutes. Whisk in chicken stock and orange juice; add papaya and banana; bring to a boil, lower heat, simmer. Reduce by half, add coconut milk and whipping cream, simmer until reduced to about 2 cups. Strain. Makes two cups.

Chicken or Beef Fajita Salad with Avocado Vinaigrette

2 Heads	Romaine Lettuce, cut into 1" pieces		12 Ounces	Frijoles Catrines
			½ Bunch	Cilantro
6	Crisp Flour Tortilla Shells, baked or fried		2	Red Bell Peppers
			1	Onion, yellow

Avocado Vinaigrette

2 Medium	Avocados, Hass		1	Chile Serrano
2 Cloves	Fresh Garlic		2 Teaspoons	Onion, chopped
6 Ounces	Red Vinegar		2 Teaspoons	Cilantro, chopped
1	Egg		6 Ounces	Olive Oil
10 Ounces	Sour Cream			Salt and Pepper to Taste

Blend avocados, fresh garlic, red vinegar, egg, sour cream, 3 ounces of water, chile serrano, chopped onions, chopped cilantro, and salt and pepper to taste. Add olive oil.

Frijoles Catrines

1 Cup	Pinto Beans		1 Teaspoon	Mexican Oregano
½	Onion		3 Teaspoons	Green Ortega Chilies
8 Ounces	Bacon, diced			Salt and Pepper to Taste
1 Teaspoon	Fresh Garlic, chopped			

Soak beans covered in water in bowl for two hours; then pour off water. Add 2 cups of fresh water. Bring beans to a boil; reduce heat and simmer until tender but not mushy. Sauté onions, bacon and garlic separately. Add to beans and cook for 15 minutes. Add salt and pepper to taste. To make spicier, optional use of 2 teaspoons chopped jalapeños may be added.

Salsa Fresca

2	Tomatoes, cubed to ⅛"		½ Teaspoon	Oregano
½	Red Onion, cubed to ⅛"		½	Lime, juiced
1	Chile Serrano			Salt to Taste
2 Teaspoons	Cilantro			

Mix all ingredients.

Meat Marinade

5 Ounces	White Vinegar		2 Teaspoons	Salt
5 Ounces	Vegetable Oil		6	8 Ounce Portions Chicken Breast, boneless and skinless, OR skirt or flank steak
10 Ounces	Water			
3 Teaspoons	Garlic, granulated			
2 Teaspoons	Black Pepper, ground			
3 Teaspoons	Mexican Oregano			

Mix white vinegar, vegetable oil, 10 ounces of water, granulated garlic, ground black pepper, Mexican oregano and salt. Marinate meat for 24 hours. If using both chicken and beef, marinate separately. Grill or broil meat over medium coals. Cut 1 bell pepper and onion in half and then grill. Use a flour tortilla shell per serving and spoon on 2–3 ounces of frijoles catrines. In a large mixing bowl, toss Romaine lettuce, 5 ounces of avocado vinaigrette dressing, grilled strips of red bell pepper and onion, and 4 ounces of salsa fresca. Place individual salad mixture portions into flour tortilla shell. Cut grilled meat into 1/2" strips just prior to serving. Place strips of grilled meat on top of salad and garnish with remaining raw red bell pepper (which has been cut into rings) and cilantro. Serves six.

SARENTO'S

Key Lime Tarts

Crust

1 Pound	Graham Cracker Crumbs		¼ Cup	Clarified Butter
½ Cup	Sugar			

Mix all ingredients until well blended.

Filling

4 Cups	Sweetened Condensed Milk		6	Sugared Egg Yolks
			½ Cup	Key Lime Juice

In a mixer, mix milk and yolks until blended. Add lime juice and mix until well blended.

Meringue

6	Egg Whites		¼ Cup	Sugar

Heat sugar and egg whites constantly stirring until sugar dissolves. Whip in mixer until stiff peaks form. Press crust mixture into round tart molds (approximately 3" in diameter). Fill crusts with filling. Bake tarts at 350 degrees for 12 minutes; remove from oven and let cool. Top with meringue. Yield: twelve tarts.

MATTEO'S

Spicy Steamed Clams Italiano

30	Fresh Manila or New Zealand Clams (cockles)		½ Teaspoon	Lemon Grass, finely chopped
1 Tablespoon	Maui Onions, small, diced		1 Tablespoon	Fresh Sweet Basil, julienned
1 Teaspoon	Garlic, chopped		1 Ounce	Virgin Olive Oil
2	Roma Tomatoes, seeds removed, medium, diced		4 Ounces	Dry Chardonnay Wine
2 Ounces	Molanari Brand Sweet Italian Sausage, casing removed and meat crumbled		12 Ounces	Clam Juice
			To Taste	Hawaiian Chili Peppers, finely chopped
1 Tablespoon	Italian Parsley, chopped		To Taste	Hawaiian Sea Salt
			To Taste	Sweet Butter

In a sauté pan, sauté onions, garlic, lemon grass and sausage in olive oil. Add clams and deglaze with wine. Reduce briefly. Add clam juice and cover. Cook until clams open, then remove to a serving bowl and keep warm. Add tomato, basil, parsley, and chili peppers to liquid and reduce slightly. Finish with salt and butter. Pour over clams and serve. Garnish with Italian parsley sprig. Serve as an appetizer.

Lacquered Salmon with Lime Black Bean Sauce

4	Salmon Steaks, 6 ounce portions	1 Teaspoon	Salt
1 Teaspoon	Sugar	1 Teaspoon	Pepper
		1 Teaspoon	Shoyu

Season salmon with salt and pepper, rub with shoyu, and sprinkle top with sugar. Heat a pan with 1 teaspoon oil. Sear salmon, placing top side down. Turn over, sear other side until salmon is done. Hold.

Lime Black Bean Sauce

½ Teaspoon	Lime Juice	1 Teaspoon	Shoyu
¼ Cup	White Wine	½ Teaspoon	Shallot, chopped
1 Teaspoon	Salted Black Beans	4 Tablespoons	Cream
1 Tablespoon	Rice Wine Vinegar	8 Ounces	Unsalted Butter, cubed
1 Teaspoon	Oyster Sauce		

Combine wine, lime juice, black beans, vinegar, oyster sauce, shoyu, and shallots. Reduce to about ¼ cup. Add cream. Reduce to low, whip in butter until smooth. Adjust seasoning.

JAMESON'S BY THE SEA

Salmon Paté

1¾ Pounds	Sockeye Salmon	2 Tablespoons	Minced White Onion
1 Pound	Cream Cheese	¼ Cup	Lemon Juice
2 Tablespoons	Sour Cream	1 Tablespoon	Salt or to Taste
2 Tablespoons	Horseradish	¼ Tablespoon	Liquid Smoke

Put all ingredients (except Salmon and cream cheese) in a blender and blend thoroughly. In a KitchenAid mixer with a dough hook, put: 1¾ pound Sockeye Salmon (canned–remove all bones, skin, and blood line) and cream cheese. Blend together until completely mixed. When mixed, add blended ingredients and thoroughly mix. Put mixture in 2 quart containers (old milk containers) and freeze. When you need Salmon Paté simply cut off the desired amount and serve with a dab of sour cream on top, chopped onion and capers. Use Diamond Soda Crackers.

Double Chocolate Bread Pudding with Toasted Macadamia Nuts, Kahlua Creme Anglaise and Kona Coffee Gelato

Chocolate Cake

1 Pound + 8 Oz.	Flour	3 Cups	Heavy Cream
⅛ Cup	Baking Soda	6	Eggs
1 Tablespoon	Salt	4½ Cups	Sugar
3 Cups	Coffee	1 Cup	Cocoa Powder

Mix dry and wet ingredients separately. Slowly combine until completely mixed. Pour into greased pans and bake at 350 degrees for 30–40 minutes or until firm.

Custard Cream

2 Cups	Cream	9	Egg Yolks
¾ Cup	Milk	¾ Cup	Sugar

Mix egg yolks and sugar together, combine with milk and cream, set aside.

Kahlua Creme Anglaise

½ Quart	Heavy Cream	10	Egg Yolks
½ Quart	Milk	3 Tablespoons	Kahlua
3 Ounces	Sugar		

Whip yolks and sugar well, set aside. Heat milk, cream and Kahlua until skin begins to form on top. Slowly whip into egg and sugar mixture until completely combined, return to stove on medium heat stirring continuously. Mixture will begin to thicken. When it reaches desired thickness, remove from heat and chill immediately.

Break up Chocolate Cake into large bowl, pour Custard Cream over and mix well. Let soak in refrigerator for 2–3 hours. Bake at 350 degrees for 20–30 minutes or until outer crust begins to form.

Macadamia Nuts
Chocolate Chips

At this time top with chopped macadamia nuts and chocolate chips. Return to oven for 5 minutes. Serve with your choice of gelatos or fresh fruits.

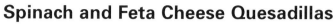

Spinach and Feta Cheese Quesadillas

Sauté together, then set aside:

1	**White Onion**	**2 Cloves**	**Garlic, Diced**

Blanch, and set aside:

1 Pound **Fresh Spinach, chopped, or ¾ pound thawed, drained frozen spinach may be substituted**

Mix together by hand:

¼ Pound	**Ricotta Cheese**	**¼ Pound**	**Feta Cheese, drained**
¼ Pound	**Cream Cheese**		

Add Onion/Garlic mix, then season with:

1 Teaspoon	**Cumin**	**½ Teaspoon**	**Salt**
1 Teaspoon	**Nutmeg**	**½ Teaspoon**	**Pepper**

Mix in spinach with hands, making sure cheese is evenly distributed throughout. Refrigerate until ready to serve. To serve: Spread 3–4 ounces of mixture onto side of 8" flour tortilla, and fold tortilla in half, being sure mixture is spread evenly across the tortilla. Place in hot dry pan, or griddle, and cook on each side until golden brown. Cut into 5 pieces, and serve with black beans and salsa, sprig of fresh cilantro as garnish. Yield: 6 quesadillas.

Banana Imu Style Fish with a Lemon Grass Pesto and Vanilla Bean Sauce

Lemon Grass Pesto

3 Cloves	Garlic		1	Large Stalk Lemon Grass, smashed and coarsely chopped
1 Bunch	Fresh Basil leaves			
1 Cup	Olive Oil			
½ Cup	Toasted Macadamia Nuts			

Place all items in a blender and process into a smooth paste. Can be stored in the refrigerator for up to one month.

Vanilla Bean Sauce

1	Fresh Vanilla Bean, split lengthwise		1	Small Cilantro Bunch, coarsely chopped
1	Stalk Lemon Grass, smashed	1 Teaspoon	Turmeric
1	Bulb Ginger, smashed	1 Cup	Rice Wine Vinegar
3 Cloves	Garlic, smashed	1 Teaspoon	Honey
1	Small Basil Bunch, coarsely chopped	2 Cups	Clam Juice
		2 Teaspoons	Cornstarch mixed with
		1 Tablespoon	Water

In a sauce pot, dry sauté first 7 ingredients for approximately 2 minutes, stirring frequently. Add vinegar and honey, then reduce by half. Add clam juice and bring to a boil. Add cornstarch mixture and thicken. Reduce heat and simmer on low heat for 20 minutes. Strain mixture through a China cap and reserve. Cut white fish filet into 2 to 3 ounce pieces. Cut banana leaf into 3 inch wide strips. Lay out strips of banana leaf and place a piece of fish on each. Spread a small amount of lemon grass pesto on each and roll in leaf. Place on grill and cook until fish is half cooked. Turn over and continue cooking until done. Time of cooking depends on type of fish used. Fish may be baked in an oven. Ladle sauce on plate garnished with rice and stir fried vegetables. Place fish on top of the sauce.

Kuau Mahi Sauté

4	**Mahi Fillets, 6 ounces each**	**4 Tablespoons**	**Salad Oil**
¼ Cup	**Chopped Macadamia Nuts**	**2**	**Large Maui Onions, thinly sliced**
½ Cup	**Shredded Fresh Coconut (or ¼ cup sweetened shredded coconut)**	**¼ Cup**	**All Purpose Flour mixed with ¼ cup cornstarch**
		½ Cup	**Teriyaki Sauce**

Prepare Teriyaki Sauce—recipe below.

In a wide frying pan, toast macadamia nuts over medium heat until golden brown stirring occasionally. Stir in coconut until toasted. Remove from pan and set aside. Add 1 tablespoon oil to pan and sate onions until soft, remove from pan and set aside. Add remaining 3 tablespoons oil to pan. Dust Mahi fillets lightly with flour mixture and add to pan and cook turning once (about 6 minutes total). Drain excess oil from pan and add onions and teriyaki sauce. Cook until sauce thickens slightly. Remove fillets to serving plates and top with onions, macadamia nuts, coconut and Teriyaki Sauce.

Teriyaki Sauce

1 Cup	**Good Quality Soy Sauce**	**5 Cups**	**Water**
1 Cup	**Sugar**	**½ Cup**	**Thinly Sliced Ginger**

Combine in a non-reactive sauce pan. Heat slowly over medium heat until surface starts to steam—just prior to boil. Let cool. Refrigerate until needed (with ginger slices left in). Makes approximately 2 quarts.

Maccheroni al Ragu D'Agnello (Short Pasta in Lamb Meat Sauce)

2 Pounds	Boneless Lamb Shoulder	1	Red Bell Pepper, cut in strips
½ Cup	Olive Oil		
4 Cloves	Garlic	1	Yellow Bell Pepper, cut in strips
	Bay Leaves		
	Salt and Pepper	1 Pound	Rigatoni or Penne Pasta
	Chili Powder		Romano Cheese
1 Cup	Sweet Vermouth (or a sweet White Wine like Chablis)		Grated Sheep Milk Ricotta Cheese (if you can find it)
			Mint Leaves or Parsley
12 Ounce Can	Crushed Tomatoes		

Slice the boneless lamb shoulder into thin strips and trim the fat. In a 2 quart pan, sauté the olive oil and garlic. When the garlic is a blond color, add the lamb strips, a handful of bay leaves, salt and black pepper to taste, a pinch of chili pepper. Brown the lamb and splash it with sweet vermouth or wine. Add the yellow and red peppers. Simmer for a few minutes and add the crushed tomatoes. Let it simmer for 2 hours with the lid on. Remove the lid for the last 15 minutes to reach desired consistency of a stew. Boil pasta in salty water for the time recommended. Mix the sauce and pasta in a big serving bowl and sprinkle with romano cheese and (if you can find it) with grated sheep milk ricotta cheese. Decorate with mint leaves or chopped parsley. Serves five.

KAMUELA PROVISION CO.

Charred Ahi with Three Bean Rice

4	Ahi Blocks, 3 Ounces	2 Tablespoons	Blackening Spice
1½ Cups	Three Bean Rice (recipe below)	1 Tablespoon	Wasabi Mustard
		2	Lemons
4 Tablespoons	Clarified Butter	4 Ounces	Soy Sauce

Dip Ahi in clarified butter. Sprinkle with blackening spice. Char all sides very lightly in very hot cast iron pan. Slice and serve over Three Bean Rice. Garnish with lemon, wasabi and soy sauce in eye cup. Serves four.

Three Bean Rice

1 Cup	Converted Rice, cooked		Salt and Pepper to Taste
1 Cup	Wild Rice, cooked	½ Cup	Kidney Beans, cooked
1 Tablespoon	Red Bell Pepper, diced	½ Cup	Navy Beans, cooked
1 Tablespoon	Green Bell Pepper, diced	½ Cup	Black Beans, cooked
1 Tablespoon	Maui Onion, diced	1 Teaspoon	Garlic
1 Tablespoon	Cilantro, chopped	3 Ounces	Cabernet Dressing (recipe below)
⅓ Teaspoon	Cumin		
⅓ Teaspoon	Coriander		

Cook rice and cool. Cook beans and cool. Mix all ingredients in large container. Add Cabernet Dressing last. Mix well.

Cabernet Dressing

3 Ounces	Soy Bean Oil	1 Teaspoon	Sugar
1 Ounce	Cabernet Sauvignon	1 Teaspoon	Corn Syrup
1 Ounce	Wine Vinegar		Salt and Pepper

Chocolate Croquant with Ginger–Vanilla Bean Sauce

8 **Macadamia Nut Cookies from Miriam's Bakery (or any good, crunchy cookies)**

Filling

1½ Cups	Cream, whipped stiff		4 Ounces	Semisweet Chocolate
12 Ounces	Milk Chocolate			

Melt the two chocolates in the top of a double boiler. Let cool slightly and gently fold into the whipped cream.

Ginger–Vanilla Bean Sauce

6	Egg Yolks		½ Ounces	Fresh Ginger, grated
2 Cups	Milk			Vanilla Extract
¼ Cup	Sugar			

Boil milk. Whisk egg yolks and sugar together. Add milk to the egg mixture. Bring to a simmer being careful NOT to boil. When sauce coats the back of a spoon, remove from heat. Add ginger and vanilla extract to taste. Pipe the filling between two cookies and place in center of the plate. Surround with sauce and garnish with fresh strawberries.

GLOSSARY

Ahi—Very popular, often served as sashimi. Ahi is the Hawaiian name for yellowfin and bigeye tuna. It is red in color when raw and turns almost white when cooked.

Aku—Is also known as skipjack tuna, and may be eaten raw as sashimi or cooked.

Cilantro*—Chinese parsley.

Coconut Milk*—Made from coconut meat and water. Available canned or frozen.

Daikon*—In the turnip family with a similar flavor to a radish.

Dashi*—Japanese soup stock.

Fish Sauce*—A thick, brown, salty sauce made from anchovies.

Ginger—A rhizome (similar to a root). Peel the outer skin, then finely chop or grate. It has a spicy flavor.

Guava—A plum size tropical flavored fruit primarily used for juices, jellies, and sauces.

Hoisin Sauce*—A sweet, spicy, fermented soybean sauce.

Kaffir Lime Leaves*—Often used in Thai cooking, they produce a citrus flavor and aroma.

Kiawe Wood—Similar to mesquite.

Lilikoi*—Passion fruit. Available in frozen concentrate form which is often used in recipes.

Lumpia*—Used to wrap egg rolls and other items.

Lychee—A delicious fruit with soft, sweet, juicy meat surrounded by a reddish woody shell that needs to be removed before eating the fruit.

Mahimahi—Dolphin fish (unrelated to the mammal). White, delicately flavored meat. Very popular.

Mango—A sweet tropical fruit that is yellow with some orange and red. In some recipes peaches may be used as a substitute.

Maui Onion—A sweet and mild onion grown in the cooler climate of Kula, Maui (the upcountry area).

Mirin*—A sweetened rice wine. One teaspoon of sugar may be substituted fo one teaspoon of Mirin.

Miso*—A thick fermented soybean paste commonly used to make miso soup which is light and brothy.

*Can be found in Asian food markets. Some items are available in Asian sections of supermarkets.

Nori*—Sheets of dried, compressed seaweed used for wrapping sushi rolls.

Onaga—A delicately flavored red snapper. Snapper, monkfish, and orange roughy may be substituted for Onaga.

Ono/Wahoo—Similar to mackerel or tuna with white, delicate, flaky meat. Often used as a substitute for Mahimahi.

Opah/Moonfish—Pink to orange flesh. Suitable for a variety of preparations.

Opakapaka—Hawaiian pink snapper with a delicate flavor and moist meat. Snapper may be used as a substitute.

Panko*—Japanese flour meal used for breading.

Papaya—A very popular pear shaped fruit with yellow skin when ripe. The melon–like flesh is sweet and mild.

Poke—Pieces of raw fish in a flavorful marinade including seaweed and sesame oil.

Pupu—Appetizer, hors d' oeuvre.

Sake*—Japanese rice wine.

Sashimi—Thin slices of very fresh raw salt water fish. Ahi is most commonly used for sashimi.

Shiitake Mushrooms*—Large mushrooms with dark caps. Available dried or fresh.

Shoyu/Soy Sauce*—A salty liquid flavoring made from soybeans.

Taro—A tuberous vegetable. Taro is a staple food of the Hawaiian culture and is used to make poi (a thick starchy paste). The flesh is a light purplish–gray. Taro is now being used by many chefs in a way similar to potatoes (chips, hash browns, etc.).

Tobiko*—Often used in sushi, it is the orange–reddish roe of the flying fish.

Tofu—White soybean curd with a mild flavor. Blocks of tofu which are packed in water (drain and rinse tofu before using) are available in most supermarkets.

Uku—Gray snapper.

Wasabi*—Similar to horseradish. May be purchased in powder form and mixed with water to make a paste. Served with sushi.

*Can be found in Asian food markets. Some items are available in Asian sections of supermarkets.

INDEX OF RECIPES

INDEX OF RECIPES

INDEX OF RECIPES

Note:

    Chefs and restaurant owners chose the recipes that they wished to contribute. Some represent items from the menu, others are specials that are served occasionally or seasonally.

    The recipes have not been kitchen tested by the author. Effort has been made to make the recipes clear and easy to follow and they have been proofread three times. Be adventuresome, experiment, and enjoy!

INDEX OF RESTAURANTS

Tasting

Paradise

Restaurants and Recipes of the Hawaiian Islands

To order more copies of this book please send $14.95 per copy to:

Coastal Images
P.O. Box 1006
Kula, HI 96790–1006

Please include $3.00 (per address) for shipping and handling. This includes up to 10 books.

Send_____book(s) to:

Name_____

Address_____

City_____ State_____ Zip_____

Send_____book(s) as a gift to:

Name_____

Address_____

City_____ State_____ Zip_____